# ESSENTIAL LE

CW01068593

# Interviewing and Counselling

Jenny Chapman

Series Editor
JULIE MACFARLANE

Cavendish
Publishing
Limited

First published in Great Britain 1993 by Cavendish Publishing Limited,
The Glass House, Wharton Street, London WC1X 9PX.
Telephone: 0171-278 8000        Facsimile: 0171-278 8080

**British Library Cataloguing in Publication Data**

Chapman, J
Interviewing and Counselling – (Essential Legal Skills Series)
I Title II Series
344.023

ISBN 1-874241-44-9

Cover photograph by Jerome Yeats
Printed and bound in Great Britain

# Contents

# Editor's Introduction

*'The essence of our lawyer's craft lies in skills ...; in practical, effective, persuasive, inventive skills for getting things done ...'*

Karl Llewellyn

The appearance of this new series of texts on legal skills reflects the recent shift in emphasis in legal education away from a focus on teaching legal information and towards the teaching and learning of task-related and problem-solving skills.

Legal education in the United Kingdom has undergone significant changes over the past ten years as a result of growing concern, expressed for the most part by the profession, over its adequacy to prepare students for the practice of law. At the same time, many legal educators have voiced fears that concentrating on drilling students in substantive law promotes neither the agility of mind nor the development of judgment skills which provide the basis for continued learning.

Today courses providing clinical experience and instruction in legal skills are increasingly a part of undergraduate law programmes. Both branches of the profession in England and Wales have fundamentally revised the content and format of their qualifying courses to include direct instruction in practical skills. In Scotland, the Diploma in Legal Practice, which emphasises the learning of practical skills, has been in place since 1980/81.

Nonetheless, legal skills education in the United Kingdom is still in its infancy. Much is to be learned from other jurisdictions which have a longer history of the use of practical and experience-based teaching methods, lessons invaluable to UK law teachers many of whom now face the challenge of developing new courses on legal skills. The ready exchange of ideas between skills teachers in the United Kingdom and abroad is an important part of the development process. So too is the generation of 'home-grown' texts and materials designed specifically for legal skills education in undergraduate and professional schools in the United Kingdom.

The introduction of skills teaching into the legal education curriculum has implications not only for what students learn in law school but also for how they learn. Similarly it has implications for the kind of textbooks which will be genuinely useful to students who wish to succeed in these programmes.

This new series of texts seeks to meet this need. Each text leads the reader through a stage-by-stage model of the development of a particular legal skill; from planning, through implementation in a variety of guises, to evaluation of performance. Each contains numerous practical exercises and guides to improve practice. Each draws on a network of theories about effective legal practice and relates theory to practice where that is useful and relevant.

The authors are all skills teachers with many years of practical experience at all levels of legal education. They draw on relevant literature and practice from all over the common law world. However each book is written specifically for students of law and legal practice in the United Kingdom and sets learning in the context of English law and against the backdrop of the Law Society's standards for the new Legal Practice Courses, due to commence in 1993/4.

Each of these texts is designed for use either as a supplement to a legal skills course taught at an undergraduate or professional level, or as a model for the structure and content of the course itself. We recommend the use of these books, therefore, to students and skills teachers alike, and hope that you enjoy them.

Julie Macfarlane
London, Ontario
January 1993

# Acknowledgements

My thanks and appreciation to Julie and Jo for their much needed patience, support and encouragement. To Rebecca for her assistance and contributions and to academic and professional colleagues and students on both sides of the Atlantic and in Australia for theirs. Finally to Nora for typing the hard copy (and it was hard) in addition to everything else she has to do.

Jenny Chapman
August 1993

# CHAPTER

## 1 The Lawyer/Client Relationship

## 1.1 The winds of change

Traditionally the lawyer/client relationship has been an unequal one, with the lawyer generally in an authoritarian and often paternalistic role. It was largely assumed that the lawyer's specialist body of knowledge entitled him literally to lay down the law: to tell the client what he could and could not do without too much concern for what the client wanted. A more benign version of the same approach is that of the paternalist, still authoritarian but now claiming to know what is in the client's best interests, assuming (or insisting upon) the course of action that she thinks best. The end result in both cases is that different options are not necessarily explained to the client, client choice is regarded as irrelevant and the lawyer takes over.

It can be a very attractive proposition for clients to hand over all their problems to a professional for a solution. This traditional form of the lawyer/client relationship has been largely self-perpetuating until relatively recently. There are a number of reasons for what is a discernible change in client expectations, for example, in relation to the process of decision-making. In the 1990s the traditional paternalistic approach of 'your lawyer (or doctor) knows best' will no longer do.

Only in the last decade or so has attention focused on the skills professionals need in addition to their mastery of a specialist body of knowledge. In particular, clients have started to insist that their legal advisers demonstrate better communication skills. Clients today are better informed, less accepting or, as professionals might say, more demanding. They want to be listened to, to know what is going on and to have some say in decisions based on information supplied by the professionals. Nevertheless, client demand for a more equal partnership with their legal advisers has not, in itself, brought about change. The impetus for change, however, can be attributed at least in part to the steady increase in client complaints; and subsequently the introduction of direct training in skills into legal education.

## 1.2    Changing expectations: client complaints

Clients are now more willing to complain about their legal advisers, evidenced by the increase in the number of complaints made against solicitors. The Solicitors' Complaints Bureau, established in 1986, reports that the majority of complaints relate to poor communication and delay. In 1990 the Bureau set up a telephone helpline service for complaints. In 1991 this special helpline received over 12,000 calls in addition to the nearly 11,000 enquiries dealt with by the Bureau's main switchboard.

The Bureau's aim is 'to strengthen and maintain the confidence of the public and the profession in the conduct and service of solicitors' (Annual Report 1991). This reflects a change in emphasis from 'discipline' to 'redress for the client' when an allegation of inadequate professional services has been made. (The Solicitors Act 1974 amended by The Courts and Legal Services Act 1990).

Also in response to rising levels of concern about lawyer/client relations, the Law Society has introduced Rule 15 of the Solicitor's Practice Rules 1990 (in effect from May 1 1992). (See Appendix A at the end of this chapter.) Rule 15 requires firms to set up an internal complaints procedure, in order to encourage dissatisfied clients to approach the firm first. Where this proves to be ineffective in resolving disputes a Diagnostic Unit has been set up to deal with Rule 15 complaints which appear to be resolvable if the client discusses the matter with the firm concerned. This has so far dealt with 957 referral letters (only 12% of which failed to be settled by the firm).

## 1.3    Skills training for lawyers

Both branches of the profession now acknowledge that in order to reach the required standard of education and training, prospective lawyers need to study more than laws and procedures. From 1993, the Law Society's professional qualifying examination (the Law Society Finals), renamed the Legal Practice Course, will include at least 20% instruction in legal skills. The Council of Legal Education introduced skills teaching onto the Bar Finals course in 1989, and that course now focuses on the skills required by barristers in practice.

Sceptics argue that skills cannot be taught and that the best way is to 'pick it up as you go along' during articles or pupillage, by observation and experience or through a vague process of osmosis. It is of course true that the practical apprenticeship and 'on the job' training plays an essential part in a new lawyer's education. There are, however, a number of disadvantages to the traditional system of training, especially where it operates without preparation or review. The most obvious is that it is based on the assumption that all experienced lawyers are exemplars of good practice in all areas. What happens to the trainee whose role model is incompetent or sets a bad example? The number of official complaints indicates that such lawyers do exist or are perceived to be unskilled by clients. Without some preparation and knowledge of an appropriate level of competence, bad habits as well as good ones may be learned. How is the trainee to discriminate? The 'throw them in at the deep end' school of training forgets that the experience itself is not enough, and is certainly less worthwhile without the opportunity for structured reflection and review.

Without sufficient training in interviewing and counselling, a trainee will often have little or no idea how to approach his or her first client interview. The trainee may establish a good relationship with the client but still fail to obtain accurate information because he or she has not learned the skill of questioning. Alternatively he may fire constant questions at the client but fail to listen and respond appropriately to the answers or, the client may come away feeling pleased with the interview, having been given reassuring (but wrong) advice. A 'good interview' must achieve some basic objectives. How is the trainee to know without an observer present to give feedback? Time and financial considerations very often make it unrealistic for the trainee to conduct an interview with a more experienced lawyer present as observer and trainer.

Clients who are on the receiving end of an unskilled interviewer are themselves providing the learning experience for the trainees. Clearly we all learn more from on-going practice and experience; however it is preferable that trainees should provide a reasonably competent service to clients from the start. This is possible if they are at least provided with the necessary tools, maps and guidelines before they start 'trying out' on the general public.

## 1.4    A competitive market for legal services

The market for legal services is now extremely competitive. Clients assume, and are entitled to assume, professional knowledge and competence in the law, and are now looking for something more in their legal adviser. What matters to clients and ensures not only their loyalty but also whether or not they will recommend you to others, is how they are treated. Are they treated with respect, listened to, kept informed and charged a fair and reasonable amount? Are their concerns understood? Clients from industry and business expect their legal advisers to have some commercial awareness so that they are able to assist such clients to achieve their business objectives. Equally, clients are more likely to feel satisfied with the legal advice they are given if there is a feeling of understanding and empathy between their lawyer and themselves.

In this competitive climate, market forces have compelled solicitors to focus on clients' needs, interests and preferences. You may be the greatest living expert in your field but if you cannot establish a good relationship with clients they will go elsewhere. The relationship extends to everyone in your firm who has contact with clients, in particular the switchboard operators, receptionists and secretaries who are usually the first point of contact, and have long been overlooked and undervalued. Solicitors are now having to learn how to manage their businesses and their staff and require a whole range of skills to do this successfully. To compete in the legal services marketplace they need to be able to communicate effectively with their clients, their colleagues and their staff. Interviewing and counselling skills are central to this process.

## 1.5    Legal professionalism in the '90s

The trend in lawyer/client relations is now clearly towards a more collaborative, symmetrical relationship. This change does not detract in any way from what it means to be a professional, but is an acknowledgment that problem-solving requires both the expertise of the lawyer and the contribution of the client.

The concept of professionalism encompasses certain ideas and ideals. Firstly, that you have reached the required standard of education and training in a specialist body of knowledge. Secondly, that you are a fit and proper person to be a member of that profession, that is, that you are to be trusted. Thirdly, a professional attitude should mean that you are committed to providing a service rather than just making a profit. In return, a professional person receives recognition, status and is generally well rewarded financially.

The duties professionals owe to clients are set by law and by their professional bodies. In the case of solicitors it is the Law Society which has statutory power to regulate its members. It does this by imposing certain requirements for legal education, by establishing a professional code of conduct, and by disciplining members who breach the code. In order to practise as a solicitor you must have a practising certificate issued annually by the Law Society, which also provides professional indemnity for claims made against its members. The grant of a practising certificate depends on compliance with the Continuing Professional Development requirements which currently apply to all solicitors admitted since August 1987, and which will be extended to the entire profession, in stages, by 1998. This compulsory continuing education includes not only substantive law, but skills and management training. The aim is to encourage solicitors to keep up-to-date and to improve and maintain standards of practice.

## 1.6    Discharging your duty of care: communicating with your client

Higher and highly specific standards of conduct are therefore imposed on professionals over and above the general standards of conduct imposed on everyone by the law of the land. For example, the law of tort imposes a duty of care on those who hold themselves out as having a specialist skill or knowledge to clients who seek their advice. Failure to reach that standard resulting in loss or damage to the client could result in a claim for damages in negligence.

Discharging the duty of care which you, as a professional, owe each of your clients depends on you developing a wide range of skills. This does not mean that all lawyers are expected to know about all aspects of law. However, you are expected to know enough not to give wrong advice and you also have a duty to keep up-to-date. This means that you must know how to conduct legal research and be prepared and equipped to do so. The starting point and major resource for research is usually your client. This means that you must be able to conduct an effective interview for which you need a range of basic communication skills including the ability to listen, question and explain.

As an example of how you might draw on these various communication skills in practice let us analyse the case of a client who wants advice about what appears to be a sale of goods matter. You will need to establish through the effective use of questions the following. Firstly, whether there was in fact a contract between the client and the seller; the date of the contract; and any evidence of the contract, for example a receipt. Secondly, whether it was a contract of sale or a contract to supply goods and services. Thirdly, whether the goods were of merchantable quality and fit for the purpose at the time of sale or supply and for how long they remained so. Fourthly, whether the client inspected them before the contract or sought independent expert advice. Fifthly, whether the client has misused the goods in any way. Sixthly, whether the client wants to return the goods, have them replaced or have them repaired.

Whether or not the client's objectives can be achieved will depend in the first place on you establishing the foregoing facts accurately. For example, a client who has not followed the manufacturer's instructions may be unwilling to admit misuse because it weakens the claim, and tactful probing about how the goods malfunctioned may be necessary. This can be surprisingly difficult because our social conditioning tends to lead us to believe what people say and we may wrongly assume that clients always tell their lawyer the whole truth. In reality, we all want to put forward the best possible view of ourselves and our case and clients may well have a tendency to tell the lawyer what they think the lawyer wants to hear. Chapter Four of this book deals in more detail with questioning techniques and gives practical advice on how to deal with situations where accurate information is difficult to obtain.

In order to obtain accurate information about misuse you will probably need to explain the law to the client. At the end of the interview, you will also need to explain what action might be taken next by both your client and yourself. How do you do it? Explaining skills are another element of effective communication. These are discussed in more detail in Chapter Two.

## 1.7    Exercise

The client tells you that her parents gave her a video camera for her birthday. She used it for the first time on holiday two weeks later and it seemed to work perfectly well at first, but the second video tape she took came out in black and white and without sound. She telephoned the shop who refused to do anything about it because she has no proof of sale. She does not want to tell her parents that the camera is faulty.

1   Formulate one or two general objectives for this interview.

2   List the questions you would ask to obtain further information.

3   Formulate some questions relating to misuse (note - be careful to avoid making sexist assumptions).

4   If she hints at possible misuse - for example, 'well, it did get a little splashed once by the pool' - how would you explain the law in order to find out further details?

5   What solutions might you suggest?

You may wish to role play this with a colleague and then discuss whether you achieved your original objective(s).

## 1.8    Lawyer/client expectations

Before moving on from the general context of the lawyer/client relationship to a more detailed examination of the skills involved in effective interviewing, it may be helpful to look more closely at the assumptions and expectations of both lawyer and client, since these can often conflict and give rise to misunderstandings.

Clients sometimes have unrealistic expectations about what their lawyer can do for them so that disillusionment is an inevitable consequence. The slowness and cost of being involved with lawyers, while often anticipated, is a mystery to many clients. Yet clients rightly expect high standards of professionalism.

On the lawyers' side, inexperienced practitioners might make the following (often erroneous) assumptions about their clients. That they will:

- always tell the truth
- know what is relevant information and what is not
- be susceptible to reason
- express themselves clearly and precisely.

It is understandable that, in the light of experience triumphing over hope, a legal adviser may sometimes feel the need to take over from indecisive clients, to cut short the information-gathering process and to rely on assumptions about the client, the truth of the matter and what is relevant or irrelevant. This may be because lawyers see the important part of the process as problem-solving and the implementation of instructions where their professional knowledge is centre-stage. There is sometimes a feeling that the lawyers would be able to get on with their work so much better if clients didn't 'get in the way'. Obviously there are difficult and demanding clients, but this sort of attitude towards clients serves only to reinforce the prevalence of the traditional paternalistic attitude where the lawyer takes over from the client, who is then expected to fade from the scene until the lawyer requires him ...

If clients do 'get in the way' it could be because the lawyer's communication skills are lacking. It may be the consequence of inadequacies in the questioning and listening process during the interview, resulting in the lawyer failing to obtain all the relevant information about the client and therefore attempting to impose an inappropriate or inadequate resolution on an unwilling client. Alternatively, the lawyer may have failed to keep the client informed or that information and advice was not properly explained and therefore not fully understood. In these circumstances it is understandable that clients whose expectations are not being met will be 'demanding'.

The interview, particularly the first interview, is therefore crucial in establishing the lawyer/client relationship. Embarking on a thorough and accurate information-gathering process and explaining and advising your client carefully and in the clearest possible terms, is obviously time-consuming. However it will prove cost-effective if the objectives of the interview (both yours and your client's) are achieved, avoiding the need for numerous follow-ups to clear up misunderstandings and ambiguities.

The lawyer has a duty to act in the best interests of his or her client and that duty begins the moment the client walks through the door. It requires the recognition of the client as the lawyer's main resource in obtaining information and in the process of decision-making. This duty is no longer discharged by the lawyer simply imposing on the client what she thinks is in the client's best interests. In a model of collaborative decision-making, the client must be clear about the options available and their likely consequences. This is a significant part of the lawyer's role in meeting the client's needs. In addition, in order to be able to act genuinely in the client's best interests, the lawyer must know as much about her client as possible and not just about the legal problem. Discharging the duty to act in the client's best interests requires, therefore, the development of a set of interviewing skills which are discussed in the following chapters. These include preparing for an interview, establishing a rapport with clients, the development of listening and questioning skills and advising and counselling skills.

Interviewing is a practical skill and therefore improves with practice. However, effective interviewing requires more than a mastery of technique. An essential element of the process of learning from experience is to review, reflect upon and evaluate that experience. To help you develop both technique and the ability to review your own performance constructively there are practical exercises throughout this book for your individual use or on which you can work with a colleague or group.

# Appendix

## A Rule 15 (client care)

Reproduced from the Guide to Professional Conduct of Solicitors 1993 by kind permission of the Law Society.

### Rule 15(1)

Every principal in private practice shall operate a complaints handling procedure which shall, inter alia, ensure that clients are informed whom to approach in the event of any problem with the service provided.

### Comments

Rule 15(1) The complaints procedure does not require to be written but if there is a complaint to the Solicitors' Complaints Bureau, you will need to establish evidence of what the procedure is, that the client and all staff knew about it and that it was followed. The important elements are that the client has recourse to a named person, not necessarily in the firm, that the complaint is properly and promptly investigated and that 'appropriate action' is taken including the nature of the investigation and the option of referral to the SCB if the client is not satisfied with the internal procedure.

### Rule 15(2)

Every solicitor in private practice shall, unless it is inappropriate in the circumstances:

(a) ensure that clients know the name and status of the person responsible for the day to day conduct of the matter and the principal responsible for its overall supervision;

(b) ensure that clients know whom to approach in the event of any problem with service provided; and

(c) ensure that clients are at all relevant times given any
appropriate information as to the issues raised and the
progress of the matter.

(3) Notwithstanding Rule 19(2) of these rules, this rule shall
come into force on lst May l991.

## Comments

Rule 15(2). The Rule requires that you tell clients who will be
dealing with the matter and another contact in the firm eg
supervising Partner or if appropriate someone in another
department who may also be involved. It is also good practice to
give the client your secretary's name and correspondingly keeping
your secretary informed of your movements and availability so that
she can do her job efficiently.

You must also ensure that the client knows both what he/she
must do next and also what you will be doing and an estimate of
both time and likely costs. You must also keep the client informed
of progress, including any reasons for delay or why the matter may
have been handed to a colleague. Information on costs and
explanation of important documents is also required.

At the end of the matter, the client should be sent written
confirmation of completion together with any continuing
consequences where necessary. The lawyer must also account for
any client funds held and hand over papers and property to which
the client is entitled, unless he wishes the lawyer to retain them on
his behalf.

The purpose of the Practice Rule is to improve the information
that clients are given especially those clients who are unused to
involvement with lawyers and the law. It is hoped that better
communication will not only raise professional standards of client
care but reduce dissatisfaction and complaints. Breach of the
standard may be a disciplinary matter ranging from a finding of
inadequate professional services to professional misconduct or
even negligence. Essentially, they are commonsense rules of
good practice.

# CHAPTER

## 2 Developing Communication Skills

*'Know thyself'*

Inscription from the temple of Apollo in Delphi

## 2.1 The importance of trust and empathy in communication

Effective communication demands a variety of active skills including listening, observing, responsiveness, questioning and explaining your views clearly and comprehensively. But what makes communication really effective is the exercise of these skills in an atmosphere of trust and empathy.

Trust assumes reliability, openness, honesty and integrity. Empathy means the ability to identify with the other person and see things from his or her perspective. It is possible to have one without the other. In the lawyer/client relationship, the client may trust the lawyer absolutely without feeling that the lawyer really understands her. Similarly, the lawyer may empathise with the client while acknowledging that she cannot be trusted.

What is important for effective communication is for the client to both trust the lawyer and feel that the lawyer has real empathy. This makes it easier for the client to open up and be honest and greatly assists the process of accurate information-gathering. Equally, the client is more likely to respond to the lawyer's explanations and advice in an atmosphere of trust and empathy, which will encourage collaborative decision-making.

## 2.2 Learning about yourself

Learning about yourself is the first step to developing empathy. If you develop self-knowledge, you will more easily be able to understand and empathise with others. This remains true even if your clients are very different from you in personality, class, culture and circumstances. Clearly you cannot ever know what it is like to be the opposite gender, or from a different ethnic background, or old (if you are young). However, you need to be aware that you, your views and values are not necessarily the norm. At the extreme end this is the root of prejudice and discrimination. In a mild form it can lead to stereotyping, the making of assumptions or that popular form of exercise - jumping to conclusions.

Developing self-awareness and self-knowledge will therefore assist you in your ability to establish a rapport and communicate effectively with others.

How do you do this? The first stage is to develop the habit of self-scrutiny and self-analysis, that is to watch and listen to yourself as objectively as possible and assess your 'performance' in as detached a manner as possible. Another strategy is to ask friends and colleagues who have been on the receiving end of an encounter with you, or who have observed your interaction with others, for frank feedback to check whether your own assessment of yourself is accurate. This may be particularly revealing on those occasions where the reaction that you received was unexpected in some way; for example, if you felt that you were being clear, calm or reasonable yet the response of the other person indicated that this was not so. (See Chapter Six, para 6.7 and Appendix G 'Guidelines for giving feedback' - to avoid the risk of losing friends.)

If video facilities are available to you, do use them. Seeing yourself on the screen lends a certain degree of objectivity but be careful of focusing too much merely on how you look and sound. Although video is also useful for revealing distracting habits or speech patterns of which you may have been unaware, for example, fiddling with your hair or the over-use of certain habitual expressions (such as 'actually' or 'I mean'), try and focus on whether the views you express and the person you see on the screen reflect the person you think you are. If there are discrepancies, analyse why this may be so. For example, do you feel more (or less) assertive, diffident or confident than you appear? Is this because of your non-verbal communication, the way you express your views or how you present yourself? What can you do to improve areas you perceive to be presenting a false impression? Do you sometimes jump in without thinking, interrupt, fail to express your meaning clearly?

It is important, therefore, to identify how you feel and what you think about things, and why, and then to analyse how these affect the way you present yourself.

## 2.3    First impressions

Psychologists have discovered that it takes approximately 90 seconds to form a first impression of someone and 55% of that view will be based on appearance. The implications of this are significant for an interviewer meeting a client for the first time, not just for the information that you gain but also the first impression you make on the client.

### Exercise

Brainstorm with a colleague or group to list the factors that contribute to your first impressions of people.

When you have as complete a list as possible, discuss the factors that weigh most heavily with you personally, how you react to them and why. This will assist you in identifying your own prejudices and biases (see next section).

Then consider what sort of first impression you might make on the client. This will help you to develop self-awareness of how you present yourself.

See Appendix B at the end of this chapter for a 'First Impressions' checklist - but note that this is not exhaustive and you may well have additional factors.

We are able to process the information gained from first impressions very rapidly using our judgment and experience to make an assessment. An out of the ordinary feature, for example, extremes in size, can be dominating and therefore distract and hinder the formation of a balanced view.

We mostly form impressions unconsciously but since they can help considerably in deciding how to react to the person and how to establish a rapport most effectively, it is worth analysing and reflecting on what you personally notice and the affect it has on you. It can help you to identify your prejudices and manage them appropriately in the interaction with the other person, who will be simultaneously forming a first impression of you.

The positive and conscious use of the information gained from a first impression can be extremely useful and help to avoid the danger of forming an opinion which may be faulty, a barrier to communication and permanent. Be prepared to adjust your views in the light of what you continue to learn about the person to avoid the danger of stereotyping.

### 2.3.1  The value of first impressions

First impressions provide clues to help you form an assessment very quickly:

- how to put the client at ease and establish rapport
- the appropriate language to use
- the level of formality to adopt

But beware the dangers of over-reliance on first impressions:

- stereotyping
- making assumptions
- making the wrong assessment.

## 2.4     Prejudice

It is an inevitable part of a person's culture, conditioning and experience to have prejudices against some and bias in favour of others. Prejudice is usually based on ignorance while bias is based on knowledge or perceived knowledge. We are more likely to favour those who share similarities with ourselves, for example common experiences of class and education and shared interests.

It is not surprising that the most effective interviews often occur where both parties share similar backgrounds or interests. Sometimes, however, a new problem arises when it appears that interviewer and interviewee share much in common and build an early rapport. For example, interviews conducted with pupil barristers showed that they were more likely to believe people who sounded well educated. It is not a coincidence that the most successful fraudsters are those who adopt titles of some sort whether aristocratic, the armed forces or 'Professor' or 'doctor', provided they have accents to match. This is another example of how unconscious bias may be exploited.

We have to accept that we will have both prejudices and biases but what we do about them is another matter. In particular we have a clear responsibility to identify the causes of any negative reactions we might have towards our clients. The first thing is to be aware of our prejudices in order that we can manage them.

## Exercise

Consider what characteristics in other people cause you to feel any of the following:

| | |
|---|---|
| Anger | Fear |
| Aggression | Hostility |
| Unease | Discomfort |
| Dislike | Inferiority |
| Superiority | |

The next question to ask is why? For example, if you feel any of the above about someone who is from a different age group or background to yourself, is this because of your own experience, or is it a result of ignorance about them and their lives, or is it just an unthinking acceptance of the views of others? If your response is based on something in your own experience, how extensive has that experience been and has it generally been negative? Have you experienced similar behaviour from others from a different age group or background? What positive experiences have you had? What was different about those?

The point is that in any encounter, someone sets the tone. We know from our own experience and observation that negative behaviour tends to breed a negative response. In the lawyer/client relationship, the basic responsibility lies with the lawyer to establish a good working relationship and this can be virtually impossible if you allow your prejudices to affect that relationship. It is also worth remembering that since everyone has prejudices, your client may have negative feelings about you as a lawyer or about your gender, age, colour, accent, appearance and so on, and that this will affect their behaviour towards you, particularly if you somehow 'confirm' their prejudices or if you react badly to the manifestation of these prejudices.

There are a number of good reasons why we should be aware of our prejudices:

• prejudices are obstacles to effective communication because they create barriers between the parties

• if we are unaware of our prejudices, we may nevertheless give negative signals through our body language and tone of voice which will not be conducive to creating a rapport. Being aware of our prejudices allows us to try to control the projection of them and develop a professional approach. This does not mean adopting a stiff and formal style, but rather not letting our feelings get in the way of doing the job properly.

• prejudice leads to stereotyping. Stereotyping is a lazy way of approaching clients and can result in all kinds of problems. Naturally, we rely on our knowledge and experience in order to make judgments about people. At its best, this skill enables us to process clues very quickly in order to decide how we can most effectively manage a particular interview. However, relying on our unconscious prejudices often results in unfair stereotyping and making inappropriate assumptions. This can lead to missing vital pieces of information, asking the wrong questions and inaccurate and incomplete information-gathering.

• prejudice may make you judgmental. Disapproval and criticism can be quite subtly revealed by facial expression and tone of voice and cause the client to feel defensive. At worst, this may lead to an aggressive response from the client or the closing down of communication altogether.

## 2.5    Creating a rapport

Effective communication therefore requires a high level of self-awareness. Self-awareness is not, note, the same as being self-conscious which, unlike self-awareness, often impedes communication because the interviewer is thinking about himself and not the client. Only once we know ourselves well - which includes knowing our prejudices and biases - can we begin to develop relationships of trust based on openness and integrity. Effective communication also requires empathy.

In order to create a rapport it is necessary to empathise with the client. This does not mean the same as to sympathise, which suggests agreement or accord, or sometimes pity. To empathise means to put yourself in the client's shoes. This is sometimes difficult for professionals to do because developing objectivity is often seen as an important part of the professional role. However, this can have the effect of creating a gap between the professional's perceived role in supplying a specialist body of knowledge, and applying that knowledge to help identify and solve the client's problem which requires understanding the client and the context of the problem. Objectivity and empathy are not mutually exclusive.

Imagine, for example, that your client is a landlord whose tenant has fallen into arrears with rent. In these circumstances, the law allows the landlord to issue a notice to quit for breach of covenant. In fact, the landlord is very anxious at the thought of the premises being left empty; they are likely to deteriorate or squatters might move in. If, as the landlord's lawyer you fail to appreciate the practical consequences in this case of the legal solution and the nature of the client's concerns, particularly in a depressed property market where it might be difficult to re-let, then your simple statement of the legal rules is likely to be less than helpful. Approaching problems with empathy allows you to find out more information because the client is more likely to talk freely and to think laterally about a range of solutions with your assistance.

If in this example, the landlord tells you that no rent has been received for six months and you reply 'why didn't you do something about this sooner?' the landlord may feel that you think him foolish and this may mean that he now feels inhibited about revealing other information in case that is judged harshly.

In order to create an atmosphere of trust and empathy, it is essential to develop self-awareness and awareness of others, to avoid being judgmental and not to assume that everyone's views and reactions will be the same as yours.

### Exercise: The Bad Interview

A good starting point for analysis and reflection is to think about your own experience of being on the receiving end of a bad interview in any context. It may have been for a university place or a job, with a teacher or tutor, doctor, bank manager or other official. Consider why it was a bad interview?

- What happened to make it a 'bad' interview? (be specific)
- how did you feel during and after the interview?

It is particularly useful to do this as a group exercise, but if this is not possible try to compare your findings with one or two others.

When you have compiled your list, turn to Appendix C at the end of this chapter for a commentary.

It is useful to identify the factors that contribute to a bad interview in order to increase your awareness of them and to take avoiding action yourself. By re-writing the negative elements in your example in a positive way you should be able to come up with a blueprint for a good interview. As a general principle, you will see that the many different elements of a bad interview can usually be avoided by a recognition of the client as an individual who should be treated with courtesy, consideration and respect.

# Appendix

 **B** Checklist of factors that contribute to First Impressions

## 1 Physical appearance

Gender
Age
Ethnic origin
Dress
Hair
Size

## 2 Attitude/demeanour (eg aggressive, friendly, nervous, upset)

Facial expression
Accent/voice
Class
Handshake
Smell (drink, unwashed, scent, aftershave)

## Comments

While these factors, in isolation or in combination, may provide vital clues in helping us to manage a client, it is also true that your reaction will affect the client. For example, it is not uncommon for a young woman to feel intimidated by older male clients since they may adopt a somewhat patronising tone or show reluctance to treat her seriously. Obviously you cannot do anything about your age and gender except to be as professional as possible and win their confidence in this matter.

This exercise is about raising self-awareness and should help you not only to avoid the dangers of stereotyping but to become aware of your own prejudices. Use the information you gain from first impressions with care in order to avoid making hasty judgments, either about the client or the nature of the client's problem.

The exercise should also help you to become aware of the impression you may have made on the client and help you to learn, with experience, the best way to manage a variety of different personalities. Self-awareness is intrinsic to the ability to establish a rapport with your client.

# Appendix

## C The Bad Interview: Commentary

The following list contains a range of observations commonly made about 'bad' interviews. These have been collected from contributions made by a wide range of people during the course of numerous sessions in which this exercise has been used.

1   What happened during the interview to make it a 'bad' interview?

You will note that most of these relate to the *interviewer*

(i)  The interviewer
  • was not listening
  • was not prepared or was disorganised
  • was nervous/unsure
  • was rude or patronising
  • showed no interest / seemed bored
  • interrogated you (using closed questions)
  • had little or no eye contact
  • made assumptions
  • did not explain clearly and sometimes used jargon
  • was impatient/rushed
  • showed prejudice (for example, asked sexist questions)

(ii)  The interview itself
  • was unstructured
  • was interrupted by phone calls etc
  • allowed insufficient time to discuss all your questions

(iii) The interview room and physical arrangements

- were awkward/uncomfortable seating arrangements
- were too hot or too cold
- you were kept waiting
- the other staff (besides the interviewer) had an unwelcoming attitude (for example, you were not helped with your coat/bags)

You may recognise many of these behaviours or occurrences or indeed have some additional ones. The point is that whatever factors are present, the end result for the interviewee is a very negative feeling.

2   How did you feel during or after the interview?

- that you have not been able to say what you wanted
- that you were not listened to
- that you were made to feel inadequate/humiliated
- that your views were ignored
- that you did not understand what was said to you
- that you were unclear about what would happen next
- that you were not treated with respect
- anxious, stressed or fearful
- upset and/or angry
- physically uncomfortable

Clearly such negative feelings are not a good basis on which to build empathy and trust.

Re-writing the negative behaviour or occurrences above in order to promote positive feelings will provide you with some practical guidelines for good interviews.

# CHAPTER

## 3 Preparing For The Interview

*'Are you sitting comfortably? Then I'll begin.'*

**Listen with Mother**
**BBC Childrens' radio programme**

## 3.1    The interviewer

You may think that a first interview requires little preparation on your part. There are no notes or file to read and you are unlikely to have more than the barest information; the client's name and some indication of the nature of the problem from your secretary or receptionist:

'Mr Knossos is coming in at 3. He has got problems with his tenants.'

Clients may misdescribe the problem from a legal perspective because they are not, after all, lawyers and will simply state their perception of what is troubling them. For example, a 'family problem' may turn out to be a man who wants to evict a member of his extended family from the matrimonial home. This obviously involves other issues such as housing as well as the family relationships. In other cases, the client may be embarrassed in stating the problem and, may, for instance, seek advice on an 'employment problem' which is subsidiary to the main issue of a summons for a criminal offence. This might lead you to concentrate on the employment issues whilst the client's main concern is the summons. Many clients are not very clear about what the problem is and will rely on you to formulate it for them from a tangle of facts and feelings. It is thus important not to go into the interview with preconceptions about the legal issues on which you may have to advise.

So how do you prepare yourself? The first thing is to try and put yourself in the right frame of mind. You should, if possible, stop what you are doing at least 5 minutes before you are due to begin the interview in order to give yourself the opportunity to clear your mind of extraneous matters and to concentrate on the task in hand. Chapter Four discusses aids to effective listening, some of which relate to your own physical and mental state. Missing meals, not getting enough sleep and worries of all kinds can affect concentration, so it is important to take a little time to relax and prepare yourself for the interview. Although this is the ideal, it is not always possible; however taking the opportunity to mentally prepare yourself mentally does help confidence when you are starting out on your professional career.

Another boost to your confidence is to look reasonably presentable, clean and tidy rather than crumpled and unkempt. Depending on the circumstances, clients may certainly feel slightly daunted by an ultra smart appearance but equally, scruffiness may lose you a little credibility and suggest an unprofessional approach. Firms with a largely commercial clientele are likely to have quite strict dress codes for their solicitors and trainees. You may think appearance is irrelevant but, as we have seen in Chapter Two, first impressions do count and the basic rule is to try and develop a sense of appropriateness in how you dress and present yourself, at least until you are so competent and confident that it really does not matter! To test the importance of appearance, notice how often you and others describe people in terms of looks or comment on their appearance.

## 3.2    The preliminaries

### 3.2.1    Office staff

The client's first contact with a solicitor is likely to be via the switchboard operator, secretary or receptionist. How helpful and approachable are your support staff on the telephone? Do they take down the essential information accurately? Do they know what information you require? For example, although they are dealing with a great many clients, it is very important to the individual and for you that you should get his/her name right. Off-hand and unhelpful staff are a major cause of complaint by clients.

It is your responsibility to ensure that you have a good working relationship with support staff. This means keeping them informed of your movements and availability so that clients can get hold of you. Secretaries find it difficult to have to report to clients continually that you are 'tied up in a meeting'. Equally, your staff should have clear instructions from you about what you require in standards of communication and accurate information when dealing with clients on the telephone and in person.

### 3.2.2  Reception arrangements

What arrangements are there for greeting clients by name, taking coats, bags, umbrellas, offering tea or coffee and generally making them feel welcome and comfortable, bearing in mind that they may be feeling anxious or apprehensive; or that they may arrive expecting a high class service because they are 'important' clients? All clients are important.

Is your reception area as pleasant and comfortable as it could be within the restrictions of space and cost? Flowers, plants, pictures, seating, reading material (for adults and children if appropriate) that is not hopelessly out of date, all help to create an impression of consideration for the client.

Does your office cater for specific needs like wheelchair access, arrangements with interpreters, a play area for children? (Some firms do now provide this.)

While it is sometimes inevitable that clients sometimes have to be kept waiting, do try and keep to the time of the appointment and make sure that they are informed if there is a delay and the likely length of it, with apologies.

## 3.3    Information and research

One question that support staff should ask clients is whether this is a first interview or not. If the client has consulted you or someone else in the firm on a previous occasion, then you will need to look at the file and if necessary consult the colleague who dealt with any previous matters which may or may not be related to this interview. This could save time at the interview and also give you useful background information. In large firms with several departments it can sometimes be embarrassing to discover during an interview that the client has already dealt with another department in the firm and expects you to know all about him or her. In such firms you may also have the benefit of a library service which can provide useful information on business clients for example, or you may want to do a company search before the interview so that you have some idea about the client's business affairs. Research into the relevant area of law will also be helpful, provided that you have sufficient information about the nature of the client's concern in consulting you.

Preliminary research may also reveal a possible conflict of interests before you become too involved with the client. It is sometimes difficult to explain at a later stage that you cannot continue to take instructions from the client because your firm is already acting for the other party. An obvious example would be where you act for a commercial landlord and a tenant in dispute also seeks your advice. Clearly there is a conflict of interests here. However in some situations the relationship may not be immediately apparent; for example, where a landlord is the subsidiary of a company for which your firm already acts, you cannot advise the tenant.

## 3.4    An interview plan

You may also wish to prepare an interview plan to help you to structure the interview. A suggested model is provided at the end of this chapter, together with a plan for an interview with a client regarding a bail application. As is the case in this particular example, some client interviews take place in less than ideal circumstances with little time for preparation, so it is worth having a plan covering the main points.

It is important to explain to the client what the structure of the interview will be, and an interview plan is useful for this purpose alone. For example, after various preliminaries to put the client at ease, and checking personal details such as name, address etc, you could say:

> 'I think we should start by letting you tell me what the problem is. Please feel that you can talk freely. As you know, whatever you say is strictly confidential which means that your visit here and whatever you say will not be made known or discussed outside this office without your permission. The rule of confidentiality applies to everyone who works here.

> When you have told me everything you want to, I will probably have to ask you some questions to make sure I have got it right and at that stage I will also take some brief notes, if you have no objection - it is much better than trusting to memory. We should then be in a position to discuss what might be done and that may be the best time to talk about fees and costs, but I can explain that now if you prefer.'

The client thus knows exactly what is going to happen and has the option to discuss fees at the outset. (See Rule 15(2), Appendix A, Chapter One.) If it is a matter of great concern to the client, she may prefer to resolve this early on in the interview. However, questions relating to income and legal aid may then arise and bear in mind that costs may also have to be discussed again when you consider possible options.

With regard to confidentiality, your explanation may need to be expanded if the client is fearful of the police, an employer, the Department of Social Security or other officials becoming involved. Thus, if you do need to contact anyone in order to obtain information on behalf of clients, it is important to get their consent, since it may mean that you will have to break confidentiality to do this.

It may be the case that the client is so desperate to blurt everything out that your plan cannot be implemented, or that the client is so reluctant to talk about the problem that you have to start with questioning rather than listening. Remember that the overall objective of the interview is to establish a rapport with the client in order to obtain relevant information to enable you to advise the client and together reach a solution. It is in each case a matter of your judgment as to the best way to achieve this objective. To stick rigidly to an interview plan which does not suit the client's needs is not recommended. Rather the purpose of the plan is to help you structure the interview and avoid the omission of essentials. It is in no way intended to be prescriptive or constricting and with experience you will become better able to develop a plan that suits your own needs and preferences.

Flexibility is vital. Interview planning can be a very constructive aid as long as you remember that the interview is for the *benefit of the client*. Your job is to make the client feel comfortable and to elicit the information you need in order to find a solution for the client's problem. Thus, adhering rigidly to your plan when it is obvious that the interview is not following the pattern you envisaged is no help to anyone. Use your judgment. Take time before an interview to think through what you need to find out and what you need to do and note it in writing, particularly if you are inexperienced, but be prepared to diverge from your plan at any time.

## To summarise

The advantages of an interview plan include the following:

- it can help you to structure your thoughts and focus on the matter in hand
- it can help to ensure that the interview follows a logical pattern
- it reduces the risk of omitting something vital
- it can encourage you to develop good interviewing habits
- it gives the client the impression that you are organised and competent.

The disadvantages of an interview plan include:

- it prevents the client from setting the agenda
- the risk of sticking too rigidly to the plan could lead you to develop a formula approach
- it can prevent the natural flow of communication.

## 3.5    The interview room

If your firm has a separate interview room or rooms, the first thing to do is to book one. Pressure for rooms can be a problem and if none is available you will have to see the client in your own office. This is likely to involve a certain amount of tidying up, since having to peer at each other through a pile of files is not conducive to a good interview. In either case bear in mind that since you will be spending a great deal of time at your office during your professional life, it is worth considering how pleasant and comfortable you can make it - for your own sake as well as the clients or indeed colleagues who come in to talk to you.

### 3.5.1    The desk

A lawyer's room is usually dominated by the desk behind which the lawyer sits. It is sometimes inevitable that your desk will be cluttered because you are working on several matters at the same time, or because of the amount of documentation involved. However, there is also a commonly held view that your busy-ness is directly correlated to the amount of paper etc on your desk. As evidence of this, a clear desk is usually taken to mean that the occupant is on holiday. In extreme cases, even holidays are not enough to shift the geological strata of papers which continues to grow over the years.

Office paperwork is difficult to control because lawyers are naturally cautious about recording everything and, having recorded it, naturally keep it. In order to establish some control over paper at the outset of your career, consider dividing everything into four piles:

1    Must keep. Papers in this category should be filed elsewhere, not on your desk.

2    For information. Read and either record if necessary (in which case back to 1) or

3    Bin it. Be ruthless: will you ever need that glossy brochure on financial advice or the latest article on restrictive covenants?

4   Send it to someone else. This could be merely a postponement of (3) above and may not help your popularity, but it may genuinely be of interest to a colleague.

Admittedly, it is harder to make judgements about some things which do not fall obviously into the above categories. This probably explains why folders and files labelled 'pending' abound. The rule would seem to be to have a regular trawl and anything you have still not read/dealt with since the last time should be binned.

### 3.5.2   Seating arrangements

Having discussed the state of the desk, let us consider the position of it in relation to seating. Lawyers invariably tend to sit behind their desks. Seats for clients or other visitors are usually on the other side of this barrier. It may well be that the space available does not allow for a different arrangement, and it may be that both lawyer and client feel more comfortable with this. It may also be that you have not considered anything more imaginative. For example, if one side of your desk is pushed against the wall you can turn and face the client without an intervening barrier. People sometimes object to 'facing the wall', but you could have a picture there, or a pinboard for useful information; and you can of course always look other than straight ahead when you are not actually writing or reading. It may take some adjustment on your part to make this departure from tradition, but it can make a psychological difference to reduce physical barriers and help the client feel that you are, literally, on his side.

The ideal would be to offer a choice according to the client's preferences, for example

Traditional arrangement

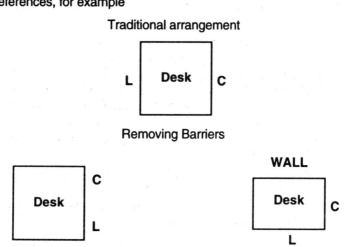

Removing Barriers

but clearly this is not always possible.

In an interview room, the same effect can be achieved by sitting adjacent to the client at the table; or at right angles rather than facing her across the table, especially if it is a substantial surface. Both the following are therefore options:

Of course, a round table solves this problem!

A surface on which to put papers, cups/glasses, and so on, and make notes is often essential, but this should not preclude the need for the most convenient and comfortable seating arrangements. It is best to have chairs of equal height rather than to have a lower seat for the client which can make him feel at a disadvantage.

### 3.5.3    Other physical conditions

If the object is to make the client feel at ease, other details to consider are:

- the temperature of the room; just because you are comfortable does not mean that the client is. You may have been sitting still and therefore feel quite cool, but the client may be hot from rushing to the interview. This can be difficult because you *both* need to feel comfortable and relaxed. The problem may be resolved by opening a window for a short time, or removing/ replacing a jacket as appropriate.

- lighting (including sunlight). You need to see each other clearly so consider the position of chairs if sunlight is streaming in, or whether your table lamp illuminates you but leaves the client in shadow.

- privacy. If external sounds can be heard during the interview then equally your conversation may be audible to those in the office, so be aware of the level of your voice.

- interruptions. Phone calls etc can be very intrusive, deflect your attention to other matters and generally distract and disrupt the interview. Unless something is genuinely urgent, you should ask your secretary not to interrupt you and, if possible, divert your phone to your secretary's number - a ringing telephone left unanswered can be very jarring.

- smoking. Many offices are now smoke-free zones and it is not unreasonable to extend the no-smoking policy to clients for the relatively short time that they are at the interview. However, it is worth considering that they may have travelled to you on public transport and that clients who are under stress are more likely to relax if allowed to smoke. If there is an office policy rather than a rule, you may want to exercise your discretion in the client's favour if it seems necessary in the circumstances. If you do, make sure you provide an ashtray.

## 3.6    Meeting your client

As professionals become more experienced they tend to forget that for some clients this may be a first time experience or at least an unusual occurrence. You therefore may need to help them to feel at ease. Do introduce yourself clearly and give them your card (if you have one) straightaway so that they know your name and status. (See Rule 15(2), Appendix A, Chapter One.)

Shaking hands establishes friendly contact - the original purpose after all was to show that you were unarmed. The usual pleasantries (journey, weather and so on) give you both time to take stock. Do not be tempted to start - or indeed end - the interview in the reception area or waiting room. These are usually fairly public places and the credibility of your assurances of confidentiality could well be jeopardised. Do make sure that the client is 'seated comfortably before you begin'.

## 3.7    Making changes

Much of this chapter has been devoted to encouraging you to look at your environment from the client's point of view. When you become very familiar with your surroundings, you grow accustomed to them and cease to be aware of how they may strike someone coming in for the first time. This applies equally to your reaction to support staff. Habits develop and often things are done because they are convenient for the people who work in that office rather than for the clients' benefit. It is worth thinking back to your first impressions of the office in order to remember how you felt. As a new trainee solicitor your aim will be to become 'institutionalised' as soon as possible; to learn systems and procedures and generally 'fit in'. You may also feel, inevitably, that you do not have the authority or the power to change things. This is true, but you can observe and note, implement your own ideas in your own space and make suggestions tactfully and diplomatically. Change can occur as a result of initiatives from below as well as from above and the way that things have always been done is not necessarily a good reason to adopt them wholesale, nor indeed to continue if improvements can be made.

# Appendix

# D Interview Plans

## A general interview plan

Although you will want to develop your own individual style, an interview plan helps to provide a structure and ensure that important aspects are not omitted. It should also help to reduce the amount of note-taking necessary during the interview. What your plan will contain will obviously depend on the amount of information that you have beforehand and the circumstances of the interview. An example of a general interview plan, and one with a client for whom you will be making a bail application, are given below:

1 Welcome the client, introduce yourself and make sure the client is comfortable (taking coat, seating etc).

2 Create an effective working relationship by explaining your role to the client and the form and purpose of the interview.

3 Encourage the client to put forward his/her views of the problem with minimum interruption at this stage.

4 Listen to what is said and observe non-verbal communication.

5 Reflect back your understanding of what has been said.

6 Ask questions to elicit facts and clarify ambiguities.

7 Give the client the opportunity to ask questions and express anxieties and respond appropriately.

8 Outline both legal and non-legal options and explain their consequences.

9 Take instructions and make clear any further action to be taken by you and the client.

10 Conclude the interview positively giving some idea of the time scale of events and the next contact (by telephone, letter or meeting).

## Interview plan for a bail application

See also *Advocacy* by A Boon in this series.

It is assumed for the purposes of this plan and for the sake of realism, that you know only the name of the client and that he is in custody in the cells of Camberwell Green Magistrates' Court charged with burglary. There are no interview rooms and the client is only brought from the police station, where he has been kept overnight, fifteen minutes before court is due to start. Despite these not uncommon disadvantages, you can give yourself a head start if you have considered the information you will need to obtain in advance.

**Note** that because of the circumstances and time constraints you will probably need to start the interview with closed questions in order to obtain details of address, age and so on. Open questions should be used later into the interview in order to find out about the circumstances of the offence.

Introduce yourself and shake hands - chat briefly.

You should now concentrate on obtaining the following information from the client:

- name and address
- lives with? (ie wife/partner/children/parents):
- working?
- age
- circumstances of the offence
- circumstances of the offender eg community ties; character; antecedents
- previous failure to appear (in answer to bail) or any offences committed whilst on bail?

Having obtained this information from the client:

- confirm any important points and clarify any ambiguities
- give the client the opportunity to ask any questions
- reassure client, whilst declining to make any promises about obtaining bail. Tell him that you will see him, in any event, after the court appearance

Section 4 of the Bail Act 1976 provides that a person to whom it applies shall be granted bail except as provided in Schedule 1.

Part 1 of Schedule 1 to the Bail Act 1976 sets out the circumstances in which a person to whom s 4 applies may be refused bail:

(a) the court is satisfied that there are substantial grounds for believing that, if released on bail, he would:

   (i) fail to surrender to custody; or

   (ii) commit an offence while on bail; or

   (iii) interfere with witnesses or otherwise obstruct the course of justice whether in relation to himself or some other person; or

(b) the court is satisfied that he should be kept in custody for his own protection, or if he is a juvenile, for his own welfare; or

(c) he is already serving a custodial sentence; or

(d) the court is satisfied that lack of time since the commencement of the proceedings has made it impracticable to obtain the information needed to decide properly the questions raised in (a) to (c) above; or

(e) he has already been bailed during the course of proceedings, and has been arrested under s 7 of the Act (arrest of absconders etc).

Paragraph 9 of Part 1 of Schedule 1 to the Bail Act 1976 lists a number of considerations to be taken into account by the court when deciding whether or not to grant bail;

(i)  the nature and seriousness of the offence and the probable method of dealing with the defendant for it

(ii) the character, antecedents, associations and community ties of the defendant

(iii) the defendant's past record for answering bail and/or committing offences while on bail

(iv) the strength of the prosecution case.

# CHAPTER

## 4    Information Gathering

*'It is the province of knowledge to speak and it is the privilege of wisdom to listen.'*

Oliver Wendell Holmes

As we have seen in the previous two chapters, the most important consideration at a first meeting is to establish a rapport with the client. An atmosphere of trust, confidence and approachability provides the best environment for getting the information you need in order to do your job effectively. You should be in control of this even if you have little or no control over the physical environment.

## 4.1    Non-verbal communication

So let us assume that you are as prepared as circumstances will allow. You are now ready to start the process of finding out what the client's problems are and how he feels about them. The first thing you will have observed is how the client appears, through a range from calm to apprehensive, tense, upset, nervous, agitated, hostile, angry and so on. This information is invaluable in helping you to react accordingly not only in the initial stages but throughout the interview, and is mainly discovered through non-verbal communication.

One reason why non-verbal communication is so important is because it is often unconscious and therefore more revealing about feelings and emotions than the content of what is said. This is attributable in part to our social conditioning, which requires us to control our emotions in public, so that public displays of emotion by adults, for example anger, may cause embarrassment or even mirth. We thus learn to control even less extreme emotions. Keeping up appearances in this way makes it difficult, sometimes, for us to express our real feelings openly. Nevertheless, as observers of human behaviour we are all fairly expert at recognising false emotion - the smile that stops at the mouth and does not reach the eyes is commonly cited - and also at recognising suppressed emotions.

Non-verbal communication has many subtle forms including body language, the attendant tone and pitch of the voice, the pauses, slowing down or speeding up of speech, and the emphasis on certain words. In short, non-verbal communication covers all the outward signs of the client's state of mind. In order to discover not only the substance of the problem but the client's true feelings about it, the lawyer must consciously take note of these underlying messages. It would be tedious and difficult without the use of visual aids to go through a list of different types of body language. However, it may be useful to look at one particular set as an example. 'Distancing' signs may include sitting with your arms folded, body turned away, head down or turned away to avoid eye contact. You can become familiar with these by observing yourself and others in situations where you feel ill at ease, for example where you dislike the other person or disagree with what is being said and therefore want to distance yourself. Note also the accompanying gestures and tone of voice.

Unless it is really obvious, physical body language forms only an element of non-verbal communication. Suppose the client is sitting facing away from you with arms folded. This could be because she is nervous, doesn't know what to do with her hands or has insufficient leg room. On the face of it, these are all distancing signs but a further vital clue would be the tone of her voice as well as the content of what is said.

Thus to obtain information about your client's state of mind, you will need to observe and listen with close attention. You should also be aware of your own non-verbal communication. Why has the client stopped talking? Is it because you are giving the impression that you have stopped listening or are not interested? Little or no eye contact, lack of other encouragement such as nodding or making 'listening' sounds (such as 'mm', 'go on'), the taking of over-lengthy notes, all tend to discourage the speaker.

Distracting habits, fidgeting and facial expressions can also be off-putting. You should also be careful to avoid using gestures which may be interpreted as threatening or indicate power. For example, it is sometimes habitual to use the hands - often holding a pen - or to point when emphasising points of speech. You should not be put off by the client's body language, but you should also be as restrained as possible yourself. This does not mean being wooden and expressionless, but being conscious of personal mannerisms which could be off-putting to others.

Aim for what is known as an open posture: sitting relaxed and upright (slouching may make you appear to be uninterested and too laid back), with your arms and legs uncrossed so that you give the impression of being open and approachable. Try and sit as still as possible and be careful about facial expressions. Appearing non-judgmental in response to what the client is saying is absolutely crucial in establishing a rapport. The most obvious way we display disapproval or criticism is by tone of voice and facial expression - the eyebrows shooting into the hairline, frowning, the pursing of lips and so on. If the client senses that you are being judgmental she may close up and be less informative. This could lead to a glossing over or dressing up of the facts, or even non-disclosure or lying since it is important for the client to feel that the lawyer will be on his side, whatever the circumstances.

In our multi-racial society, it is important to be aware of misinterpreting body language which can be harder to read if one is ignorant of what is considered appropriate behaviour in other cultures. You should be wary of making assumptions based on your own social conditioning. Eye contact, for instance, is assumed to be a positive sign of willingness to communicate in the West but may be avoided in some cultures where it may be considered disrespectful or immodest or inappropriate depending on the circumstances; for example it is not uncommon to find that some speakers will not look at the listener until they have finished speaking.

You may feel reluctant to respond to non-verbal behaviour in case you have misinterpreted it, or think it is better ignored as it could be uncomfortable or embarrassing for both you and the client. However, there is a danger that you may both miss something important by way of facts or content and also ignore the client's feelings about this. Even if you have misinterpreted the non-verbal clues, by reflecting back on these the client is likely to be encouraged to open up about the true feelings expressed:

| | |
|---|---|
| Lawyer: | 'You sound as if that upset you?' |
| Client: | 'No, not really. Well, in a way I suppose. It made me lose my temper.' |
| Lawyer: | 'What happened then?' |

If you fail to check ambiguous non-verbal clues your interpretation can only be speculative and any inaccuracies remain uncorrected. These may affect your evaluation of the problem and therefore impede the giving of appropriate advice. Bear in mind also that you are probably more experienced than you think in assessing non-verbal behaviour from day-to-day communication with others. This continual assessment of the behaviour of others happens all the time and therefore may not operate overtly or consciously. Listening, observing and reflecting consciously will raise awareness so that we become more experienced and perceptive and also learn about our own reactions to the feelings expressed.

Suppose your reaction to the behaviour is negative in some way? A good example is weeping. Social conditioning in some cultures encourages the view that people who cry have 'lost control'. A person who starts weeping in front of another will often apologise and make great efforts to stop because it is thought that the observer will be embarrassed. Consequently we do not become skilled at dealing with extreme displays of emotion like weeping.

So how should the lawyer deal with tears? Firstly, by assurances that it is perfectly acceptable to cry; that the client will not lose your respect by this apparent loss of control because you do not perceive it as such but as a normal human expression of emotion. Secondly, by an unobtrusive demonstration of your sympathy and understanding. Provide some tissues, a glass of water, cup of tea or whatever is practicable.

Should you touch the client? There is a view that prescribes that the lawyer should never touch the client except in a formal way by a handshake at the start and end of the interview. This is either because it is considered 'unprofessional' or because of the risk that your motives for touching may be questioned.

My own view is that depending on the age, gender, perception and inclination of the lawyer in relation to the client some minimal physical contact - such as a hand placed on the shoulder, or the arm, of the distressed client - may be a perfectly appropriate response and promote empathy. The important thing is to avoid showing your discomfort and embarrassment by an inappropriate response such as exhortations to 'cheer up' or 'calm down' or worse still attempting to joke or reminding the client of time constraints. It is not appropriate to ignore the tears and try to continue the interview. You may feel that the best way to handle the situation is to ask if the client would like to be left alone for a short time, or indeed for you to leave the room explaining that you will be away a little while. This indicates a sensitivity to the client's feelings by not wishing to add to the discomfort of the situation with your own unease and uncertainty of how to handle it. A few minutes in private allows the client restoration time so that the interview can continue.

It would be tactful at this stage to ask if the client feels like continuing and if so to summarise what has gone before. However, if the client would prefer not to be left alone the lawyer's role may well be to sit quietly and calmly and not attempt to 'talk away' the tears. Silence is always an option. It is impossible to provide a blueprint since the appropriate response would depend on many variables and your own perceptions and assessment of the situation.

### 4.1.2   Summary: Non-verbal communication

- adopt an open relaxed posture (but not too laid back)
- sit still and try to avoid distracting gestures
- be conscious of your own facial expression and tone of voice so that you encourage rather than discourage communication
- try to become aware of your own body language without becoming worried and self-conscious
- observe the client's non-verbal communication very carefully, and try to respond appropriately
- listen to how things are said as well as to the content.

## 4.2   Active listening

Hearing and listening are two distinct activities. We are constantly assailed by a variety of sounds which we hear consciously and unconsciously. Unusual sounds, loud noises, the mention of one's name or something which is of interest will usually cause us not just to hear but to listen, to 'switch on' or 'prick up our ears'. Hearing is merely an acceptance of sounds, often while thinking of something else, while listening is a positive activity and it is an essential skill to learn for interviewing.

The first step to learning active listening is to consider the barriers that prevent us from really concentrating. It is surprisingly easy to switch off and start thinking of solutions in response to something particular the client has said, for example,

'The tenants haven't paid rent for three months'.

Immediately you start to think about breach of covenant and eviction procedures. Lawyers tend to respond to client expectations that they should know the law and therefore may make assumptions or jump to conclusions which are dictated by the law rather than by what the client wants. While you are worrying about notice periods and so on, you may be missing vital information from the client. Thinking of what you are going to say is a barrier to concentrating on what is being said.

Other things that get in the way of active listening are related to your physical and mental state. Tiredness, boredom, anxieties, preoccupation with other problems, stress, hunger and other physical discomforts. If possible, try to spend a few minutes beforehand in order to prepare yourself mentally for the interview by relaxing and clearing the mind so that you can concentrate despite physical and mental distractions. (See also Chapter Three at para 3.1.)

Other barriers arise from external circumstances. Try and avoid interruptions from the telephone and other people. Distractions from the client, for example, physical appearance or mannerisms need to be overcome by focusing your attention away from the distraction. Once you have developed and practiced active listening, your ability to concentrate will improve because you will be able to focus on the relevant rather then being distracted by the irrelevant.

Active listening may be demonstrated in two ways. The first requires an apparent passivity: the minimum of interruptions accompanied by encouraging sounds and signals such as facial expression, eye contact and nodding to show that you are interested. This is often appropriate for the first stage of the interview and whenever the client needs to feel free to tell you the story in her own words. It is crucial to information gathering because it provides the lawyer with the opportunity not just to hear what is being said but to concentrate fully on the content and observe the non-verbal signals that show the feelings that are being expressed. If possible, avoid taking notes during these occasions since that could well be inhibiting. There should always be time later to ask questions and then take notes.

The second form of active listening requires the lawyer to use paraphrasing and key word repetition to demonstrate listening and comprehension to the client. Once this has been done, the interview can move on to a new point, the client having been satisfied that the previous point has been noted and understood by the lawyer.

| Client: | 'Well things haven't been going too well for us lately. He was made redundant last April and he has been staying out late and drinking a lot and...well, he has been taking it out on me.' |
| Lawyer: | 'He has been taking it out on you?' |
| Client: | 'Yes, well you see he hits me...He never did before...I know it's the drink - so that's why I've come to see you.' |
| Lawyer: | 'I am really sorry to hear that. Did he hurt you?' |
| Client: | 'Not badly - I am a bit bruised but I am not sure about any of it any more.' |
| Lawyer: | 'Yes, I can understand that. Now, let's see, your husband was made redundant last April and now he has started hitting you when he is drunk - how long has this been going on?' |
| Client: | 'Just the last three or four months really but I've had enough, I want it to stop.' |
| Lawyer: | 'Well, we can stop him by using what's known as an injunction. We can apply to the court very quickly to stop him from coming to the house. Is that the sort of thing you have in mind at the moment?' |

## Active listening exercise

You may find it helpful to role play this with a colleague and discuss the following points:

1 Identify how the lawyer establishes empathy with the client.

2 How is active listening demonstrated?

3 Why do you think the lawyer chose to summarise the information at that point?

4 Do you think the lawyer's analysis of the immediate legal problem was effective? (See Appendix E at the end of this chapter for a commentary.)

### 4.2.1   Summary: Listening skills

Active listening:

- requires concentration and patience. Don't make assumptions or jump to conclusions
- be aware of barriers to active listening and try to eliminate or minimise them
- demonstrate your attention by non-verbal signals
- repeat key words and phrases to show active listening and encourage further information
- summarise and reflect back what has been said. This allows the client to add, amend or clarify. Then make a note.

## 4.3   Questioning skills

It is self-evident that in order to get answers one needs to ask questions. But how, what and when we ask particular types of questions is not always so obvious. Apart from the type of question, it is important to think about the manner in which it is phrased. That is, not just the language and construction but whether the question is ambiguous or the reason for asking it not clear to the client.

For example, in order to prepare for a bail application, the client will need to be asked where and with whom she lives. On the face of it, this personal information may appear irrelevant to the defendant and needs to be explained in relation to the factors which will influence the court in granting bail, such as establishing community ties. The best principle is always to explain why you are following a particular line of questioning if it is sensitive or might appear obscure to the defendant. This should encourage a helpful response.

### 4.3.1   Open questions

The client's own narrative, while possibly rambling, ambiguous or unstructured provides a good starting point for the flow of information, and to encourage this it is often necessary to use open questions, that is, those that do not intrinsically demand a specific answer. Open questions give clients the opportunity to state the problem in their own words. This also gives the lawyer the opportunity to assess the client; is the client a 'rambler', articulate, truthful , likely to be a good or bad witness? Examples of open questions are 'what happened next?', or, 'how did you feel about that?', or, 'what did you do then?' An additional strategy is to repeat a key word or phrase as shown by the words 'He has been taking it out on you?' in the previous section (see para 4.2 above).

When you have asked an open question, do give the client the opportunity to think before following it up immediately with another question. Provided you have created the right atmosphere in the initial stages of the interview, the client should respond freely to open questions and not feel reluctant or inhibited. The lawyer's task is to listen attentively and avoid the temptation to interrupt at this point, even if the client is rambling or unstructured, or questions leap to mind in order to clarify points.

Although the lawyer may be anxious about time constraints and therefore want to get on with fact finding, it is often more productive to let the client set the agenda. An open question at the start of the interview, and where appropriate throughout, will reveal what is of importance to the client. If the lawyer leaps in too readily with closed questions, particularly if they are based on assumptions about the true nature of the problem, then it will become much harder for the client to reinstate his concerns. The danger of this is that since the focus has shifted to what the lawyer wants to know rather than what the client wants to say, if the lawyer fails to ask certain key questions, the client may forget or ignore important facts since he has lost the initiative.

### 4.3.2   Closed questions

Of course there are exceptions to this. There may well be clients who for reasons of shyness, lack of confidence or perhaps whose first language is not English will need to be started off with closed questions. Closed questions may also be used to focus a client who rambles, or to check or clarify information already given.

Closed questions are so called because they direct a 'yes', 'no' or specific response. For example,

'When did this happen?'

'Were you cautioned?'

'Have you being paying rent?'

'How old are your children?'

The chief purpose of closed questions is to clarify and obtain detailed information, once you have an overview. In addition, where the client needs some help in getting started, closed questions can often ease them in, to be followed up later by open questions.

| Lawyer: | 'Well Mr Shah, how can I help you?' |
| Client: | 'Well um, ah...(pause.)' |
| Lawyer: | 'You mentioned on the telephone that you had received a letter from the Home Office about your immigration status. Do you have it with you?' |

Once a rapport has been established, it is usually taken for granted that even if you ask a closed question the client will respond more broadly, for example with a 'yes, but...' or 'no, but...' type of answer which expands the specific answer that was required by the closed question. Unrelenting use of closed questions accepting only 'yes', 'no' or very specific answers is unlikely to build rapport. Barristers demonstrate the art of closed questioning when they particularly want to pin down a witness to a specific answer without any 'buts' or explanation: 'Please just answer the question - yes or no'. Anyone on the receiving end of a series of closed questions can feel very frustrated.

As the interview moves on and the lawyer has begun to assimilate the information, it may be appropriate to ask closed questions to clarify facts and to ensure that the information is accurate. Closed questions can be particularly useful in the following circumstances:

- to direct and control ramblers. The danger with ramblers is that over-control may prevent the discovery of vital information in the seemingly irrelevant waffle, while under-control may lead to confusion and time wasting. It is a question of judgment when you decide to close in and attempt to put some structure on the wealth of information you are given. Ramblers may well ignore closed questions and start adding lengthy explanations so it will be important for you to explain why you want concise answers.

- to deal with clients who are economical with the truth. It is a difficult lesson to learn that clients do not always tell the truth, the whole truth and nothing but the truth. The client wants to feel the lawyer is on his other side and therefore may hide or merely hint at information that is damaging to his case or self esteem so that the lawyer will not disapprove or withdraw support. Others just convince themselves of the rightness of their version, as anyone who has attempted to mediate in a dispute between friends or attended a trial will know. Each side is absolutely convinced that their version is true and the other has got it wrong.

In these situations it is vital for you to gain the client's confidence by explaining that you cannot represent him without knowing all the facts. You may also want to reiterate assurances about confidentiality, and of course make sure that your behaviour is non-judgmental, however you may feel. Closed questions, to check the information already given, followed by an open question to encourage a new version or the addition of information by the client may be the best tactic. The essential thing is to recognise the situations where you do need to test the information and not just accept unquestioningly what the client tells you.

### Exercise Two

As a demonstration of the use of open and closed questions, you may want to try this exercise with a colleague.

1   Take it in turn to be the questioner.

2  For the first part of the exercise the questioner asks the other to give information about a car accident, using **only closed questions**. The respondent must answer the question asked without amplification. Remember that closed questions direct a yes/no or one specific answer, for example 'what type of car was it?', 'what time did the accident happen?', 'was anyone injured?'

3  In the second part of the exercise, the questioner has to find out about the same incident but using **only open questions**.

4  Spend about five minutes on each interview and then compare notes. Discuss the advantages and disadvantages of each type of questioning style and how you felt about your role in each case.

### 4.3.3   Summary

Open questions

Advantages:

- encourage clients to open up
- allow clients to choose the topics of importance to them rather than what they think the lawyer wants to know
- allow the lawyer to gain an appreciation of what is on the client's agenda and a feel for the problem
- obtain insight into what is most important to the client and how she feels about things
- encourage recall of events and expression of feelings without the interruption of having to fill in detail
- ease clients into discussing sensitive or difficult issues
- provides the opportunity to observe, listen and assess the client

Disadvantages:

- can encourage rambling
- may only provide an over-view and insufficient detail; therefore the lawyer needs to concentrate on both listening to the narrative and deciding which areas to explore further
- with complex issues, the client may not know how or where to begin and what the relevant focus should be

Closed questions

Advantages:

- help to provide specific detail and clarify the information
- help to direct the reluctant client
- help to direct and control the rambler
- assist specific memory recall

Disadvantages:

- can turn the interview into an interrogation
- valuable information may be lost if the client has not been given the opportunity to set the agenda
- valuable information may also be lost if the lawyer fails to ask key questions and relies on assumptions which may in fact be false

### 4.3.4   Questions to avoid

**Leading questions** are so called because the answer is prompted and directed by the question. The main danger here is of putting words into the client's mouth, since they are essentially statements requiring confirmation, parading as questions. Directing the client's answer in this way means that you are controlling what information is given and a co-operative client could unwittingly lead you astray. For example,

'so your wife and children first came to England in June 1990?'

If the client replies 'Yes' you may fail to discover that not all his children came to England in June 1990. This leading question is based on the assumption that the family arrived at the same time.

The same question put in a different form, for example,

'When did your wife first come to England?'

'What about your children?'

will give you a better chance of obtaining accurate information.

You should also try to avoid asking **multiple questions**. Multiple questions occur either because the lawyer has thought of several points that require answers, or as a result of a belated attempt to improve or phrase the question in a different way. For example,

'How long has your family been here?. That is, can you tell me when they first arrived and did they all travel together?'

The difficulty for the client is which question to answer first, and the problem for both lawyer and client is to remember what all the questions were. This could lead to omissions or having to repeat parts of the original multiple question, which wastes time and may also lead to confusion.

Try to avoid **long complex questions** with sub-clauses, double negatives etc; a variation of the multiple question. For example,

'Would it be wrong of me to assume that, your wife and children, having entered the UK in June 1990, you then tried to make arrangements, not unreasonably, for your two eldest children to follow?'

In addition to the problems caused by multiple questions, the client may find this type of question very hard to follow and not know how to respond.

Finally, be wary of the tone of **'why' questions** which can sound judgmental if they imply that the client was foolish or unreasonable for example, 'why did you do that'?

### 4.3.5   Summary: Questioning skills

*   use both open and closed questions as appropriate during the interview.
*   give the client time and space to answer open questions especially at the start of the interview.
*   use clear concise language and avoid jargon.
*   avoid obscure, complex, multiple and leading questions.
*   if necessary, explain why you are asking particular questions.

## 4.4    Finally - a note on note-taking

Do keep note-taking to a minimum during the interview itself, concentrating on detailed information such as dates, names, addresses and so on. A fuller note can be made after the interview while things are still fresh in your mind. Although taping the interview may seem a good idea, there must be very few lawyers (or their secretaries) who have the time to transcribe a taped interview, and the presence of a tape recorder could be inhibiting to the client.

It is sensible to explain to the client at the start of the interview that you will be taking some notes in order to make a record of essential information and what advice has been given. Reassure the client that the confidentiality of the interview extends to the notes. It may seem obvious to many clients that you will be recording the interview, but bear in mind that a person charged with a criminal offence, for example, may need an explanation since his previous experience of note taking is likely to have been in a police station following a caution '... anything you say will be taken down and may be given in evidence'.

Your note should record the date and time of the interview, including both starting and finishing time; those present; the relevant information obtained from the client; what information and advice you offered: the action to be taken by you and the client and, finally, the next contact.

An attendance note is important firstly as an aide memoire. In a lengthy ongoing matter, you will be unlikely to remember exactly what was said at previous interviews. This applies equally to telephone conversations which should also be noted on the file. Secondly, it helps to avoid dispute over what advice or information you gave. Finally, a record of the amount of time spent on a matter is essential in drawing up the bill.

# Appendix

## E Active listening exercise: Commentary

### 1 Establishing empathy

Assuming the appropriate non-verbal signs eg tone of voice and body language, the lawyer shows concern for the client in the content of responses - 'I am really sorry to hear that, did he hurt you?' 'Yes, I can understand that'. Also by appreciating the need for speedy action.

### 2 Active listening

This is demonstrated by repetition, for example, 'taking it out on you' and also by key word repetition in the summary, for example, 'redundant', 'hitting', 'drunk'. Note that listening without interruption may be important when the client is explaining 'taking it out on me' since recalling painful experiences is not always easy and the client should be given time for this.

### 3 Summarising

The client's response 'I am not sure about any of it any more' is ambiguous and therefore the lawyer needs to test exactly what the client means. The client's response to this makes it clear without excluding longer term solutions which the lawyer should pick up when the immediate problem has been discussed. The lawyer does in fact leave it open by saying 'Is that the sort of thing you have in mind at the moment?'

### 4 Analysis

Having established that the client wants the violence to stop, the lawyer explains the use of the injunction, followed by further probing to discover if that would be the most appropriate remedy for the client since it clearly involves separation, at least temporarily. Obviously other relevant information will need to be sought regarding children, financial support etc before any solution can be decided upon in either the short or long-term. By failing to listen actively and give the client the opportunity to explain the substance of what is said, a lawyer may jump to the conclusion that she wants an immediate divorce.

# CHAPTER

## 5 Advising and Counselling

*'Advice is seldom welcome; and those who want it the most usually like it the least.'*

Earl of Chesterfield (1694-1773)

## 5.1 Introduction

The importance of developing effective listening and questioning skills becomes evident at the advice stage of the interview, since without the relevant information (which includes facts and feelings) you will not be able to offer appropriate advice and counselling to clients. It is all too easy for lawyers to focus exclusively on the legal issues and make assumptions about the nature of the client's problem. In developing the lawyer/client relationship it is desirable for lawyers to take a holistic approach, that is, to deal with the person not just the legal problem in isolation. This inevitably means that lawyers have to take on a counselling role as well as that of legal adviser.

## 5.2 Counselling

What exactly is counselling? The term may have negative connotations for you if it suggests merely a sentimental effusion. It may be helpful to think first about what counselling is not.

Counselling is not simply 'tea and sympathy', nor is it taking over the client's problems and dispensing advice of the 'if I were you ...' type; you are not experiencing the client's problems. Effective counselling must be non-directive and client-centred. Therefore the lawyer as counsellor assists the client in reaching solutions which are best for that individual.

The principles underlying client-centred counselling for lawyers are

- interest and empathy on the part of the counsellor
- a non-judgmental attitude ('unconditional positive regard')
- an objective non-directive attitude

This approach ensures that the client retains the freedom of choice and responsibility for the consequences of action and does not surrender these to the lawyer. This does not mean that the lawyer opts out but that the decision-making process is collaborative with each playing his or her own role. Playing the role of lawyer, you must be sure that the client has understood your explanations of all the options and their consequences and that your advice is based on what you believe to be in the client's best interests. Ultimately the client must decide upon what happens next (see also para 5.7 below).

The analogy of 'informed consent' in advice and decision-making about medical treatment is a useful one. A doctor must explain the treatment options available and the various side effects and risks, so that the patient is informed of all the facts before consenting to the chosen treatment. Failure to do so could amount to negligence if the patient suffers damage from treatment on the grounds that he or she would not have consented had all the facts been known. Equally, in the lawyer/client relationship it is important for the client's decision to be based on an appreciation of all the options and their likely consequences.

It is true that economic considerations may be relevant. For example, in medical treatment the best remedy may not be recommended by the doctor because it is too expensive. Equally, a client who is not legally aided may well choose a less desirable option because of the costs involved. When deciding whether or not to embark on litigation, it must always be considered whether this is going to be an economically worthwhile option.

## 5.3    When should advising and counselling begin?

At a first interview, the main emphasis will be on establishing what the problem is and how the client feels about it. You may not be able to offer detailed advice without some further action being taken by you (for example, the necessary legal research) and/or the client (for example a client landlord obtaining an estimate for repairs). Time is also needed for you and the client to think about possible solutions.

Therefore in most cases a subsequent interview or letter of advice would probably be necessary. Nonetheless, the client will expect some response from you today, before the first interview is concluded. The client should end the interview with a clearer understanding of what the problems are, some possible outcomes or solutions and a feeling that he or she has been listened to, understood and treated with respect.

Since you will spend much of the interview extracting information, it is important for the client to feel that you will provide some information in return. The relevance of this information will of course depend on how successful you have been in the first stage of the interview. On these foundations you and the client can continue to build up as full a picture as possible.

## 5.4   Testing understanding

It is important that before progressing to the advising stage you ensure that you have understood the client's problems and that the client understands what has already taken place. Probably the best and easiest way of doing this is to summarise your understanding of the facts giving the client the opportunity to add or amend.

Continuing with the example from the previous chapter, let us imagine that a client has come to see you because she is having matrimonial difficulties. You have managed to elicit that the reasons behind this are her husband's redundancy, drinking and his assaults on her. You have mentioned a legal remedy in terms of an injunction and you have made enquiries about alternative accommodation for one or other of them and suggested the non-legal option of marriage guidance. Before you go on to discuss the various options in detail and help the client to come to a decision, you need to be sure that you have the facts right and that the client understands what options are open to her:

'Well Mrs Wilkins, you have been very helpful in answering my questions and we are now in a better position to think about what you can do to improve the situation. I have mentioned a number of options to you such as an injunction to prevent your husband entering the home, or perhaps a temporary separation coupled with marriage guidance. Is there anything further that you would like to ask me at this stage?'

This gives the client the opportunity to ask for clarification of the various options outlined, which means that you can move on to discussing the alternatives available. For example, she will probably want to know what to do if her husband ignores the injunction. A brief summary at this stage gives the client a chance to venture more information, such as the fact the she may be considering a divorce, which will open up a whole new line of information-gathering, advising and counselling. It is far better for you to encourage the client to open up all possibilities, including those you have not thought of yourself, than to assume, with the knowledge you have as a lawyer, that the client will want to choose 'obvious solutions'.

Observe the client's non-verbal behaviour carefully while you summarise. This can provide clues as to whether or not you have got it right. From the client's point of view, the issues should be clear but still recognisable in terms of her original description of them, and not transformed by the lawyer into purely legal issues.

Your accurate assessment of the client should help you to summarise, explain and advise in the most appropriate way and thus avoid the dangers of appearing either patronising or obscure. You should always be as clear as possible to avoid any misunderstanding. Your client may be reluctant to tell you that she does not understand the particular point that you have been making and this could lead to confusion and embarrassment later on.

This last point is particularly true of jargon. Although jargon is not the lawyer's preserve and everybody uses their own forms, 'legalese' can cause particular problems. Some legal terms are in common usage without being fully understood; for example, the difference between being sued and being prosecuted; a remand on bail; searches in conveyancing; the distinction between a lease and a licence to name but a few. The important thing is to be aware of those words which have a technical meaning which is so familiar to you as a lawyer that you barely recognise them as jargon. Take care to explain exactly what you mean when you use those words.

Equally, it may be your client who uses jargon to describe specific aspects of her own field of work or expertise, or indeed just uses an ordinary word in a different sense from you. You may think that your client will expect you to know and you will therefore lose face by asking for an explanation. However it is more likely that the client will be pleased to have the opportunity to do so and you will learn more about the client's world than by guessing or making assumptions as to meaning.

### Exercise One: Clear explanations

The object of this exercise is to raise you awareness of your use of jargon. Working with a colleague or in a small group, take it in turns to explain 'how to do' something practical; a particular skill, hobby, game or sport, preferably one with which your listener is unfamiliar. The speaker should assume that the listener has minimal knowledge of the subject, and should speak without interruptions from the listener.

Spend about 5 minutes each on this and then turn to the Appendix F at the end of this chapter for feedback questions and commentary.

## 5.5    Identifying possible courses of action and explaining the legal and non-legal consequences

This is the part of the interview where it is the lawyer's turn to do most of the talking. Hopefully you have by now extracted all or most of the relevant information from the client about his case and you now have to explain to the client what choices are available and the possible consequences of those choices.

It is important to remember that the client is likely to be very concerned about the consequences of any action that he takes, particularly if there are likely to be repercussions which will have a direct effect on his life or the lives of others involved. For example, your client may wish to leave money in his will to an illegitimate child whose existence is unknown to his family. Rather than name the beneficiary in the will itself, which could cause pain and distress to his family, he might prefer to set up a secret trust in order to protect the legacy. Or your client may be suffering violence at the hands of her husband but is reluctant to have him legally removed from the matrimonial home since she believes that it is in the best interests of her children that their parents continue to live together, or she is unclear about how a separation would affect herself and the children financially.

In the majority of interviews there are bound to be considerations outside the bare legal bones of the problem which the lawyer must identify and address in order for the client to feel satisfied with the outcome of the interview. It is no good telling the client in the second of the two examples above that an ouster injunction is the answer when she has told you that it is not what she wants. It may be that she will change her mind after some counselling and further explanation of concepts such as maintenance and access, but in order to help her decide you have to recognise and deal with the non-legal consequences of any action she is considering.

To take another example imagine that your client is the landlord of a residential property. Mr Knossos rents out a house which was left to him in his aunt's will. He has his own house in another part of London. His tenants, who are students, have refused to pay the rent for the last two months because they say that the house is in a dreadful state of disrepair. They say that they will continue to withhold rent until the repairs are carried out. Your client is retired, does not have a great deal of money and the rent is a useful boost to his income. He would like to sell the house but he is worried that in order to do so he would have to sell it at less than its value and further, that he would not know how to invest the money. He does not object in principle to making repairs but he is worried that it might cost a lot of money.

Lawyer:     Well, Mr Knossos, it seems to me that you have a number of choices:

1 You can find out how much the repairs would be likely to cost and then decide if you want them carried out or not;

    (a) you could then pay for the repairs to be carried out and approach your tenants to pay back the rent owing to you;

    (b) you could pay for the repairs to be carried out and either negotiate through a lawyer or begin proceedings against your tenants for the rent;

    (c) you could refuse to have the repairs carried out and take your tenants to court for the rent owing to you and for their eviction.

    2   You can take no action at all.

Mr Knossos: I don't think I want to go to court.

Lawyer: OK. I can understand that. However, if you should refuse to have the repairs carried out, your tenants may want to take you to court to make you carry out the repairs. If that were to happen, you would be able to counterclaim for the rent owing to you; that is you would be able to make a claim for the rent as part of your defence to your tenants' claim.

Mr Knossos: Oh dear, I wouldn't want that to happen, just to get the rent.

Lawyerr: So, what do you think you want to do?

Mr Knossos: I don't mind doing the repairs as long as I get the rent.

Lawyer: Well, suppose you find out how much it would cost for the repairs to be carried out. Perhaps than you could negotiate with your tenants on the basis that you will have the repairs done if they pay the rent.

The lawyer should aim to ensure that the various courses of action and their consequences, both legal and non-legal, meet the client's goals.

## 5.6   Identifying client goals

It is to be hoped that in the course of questioning the lawyer has managed to determine the client's goals and can then proceed to help the client come to a decision by using a combination of legal knowledge and knowledge of the client wants. There may be occasions, however, where it is very difficult to determine exactly what the client wants; the client may not know himself or may be obtuse when it comes to answering questions. In such situations the best course of action is to ask the client exactly what it is that he is looking for by way of a solution. Where would he like to be by the end of this process? What will have changed about his situation and how?

Invariably the legal dimensions of the client's problem are just one small part of the wider context. The legal dimensions are not necessarily paramount in the client's mind. For example, a commercial client who wants to expand seeks your advice about purchasing a business. There are two ways she might do this; one is to purchase a company and the other is to purchase shares. You will need to advise the client about the advantages and disadvantages of each method, in addition to dealing with any property, employment and tax matters involved. The client's main interest will not be in the legal steps and documentation concerned but in a speedy and cost-effective transaction to allow the business acquired to operate as a going concern.

As well as having positive aspirations or goals, clients are also likely to have anxieties relating to their position. Part of the lawyer's task in defining clients' goals is to discover what their worries and concerns are. Often one of the clients' goals will be simply to alleviate that anxiety.

Be careful about brushing aside what may appear to you to be trivial or peripheral concerns with a brisk, 'don't worry about that' response without explanation. You may be dismissive from the best motives because your legal knowledge and experience tell you that it is either an easily solved problem or of no great significance compared to the main issue. Imagine that your client has been made redundant and is appealing on the ground of unfair dismissal and has not received a reference promised by the employer. You may be concentrating on the facts needed for presenting the case at tribunal and the question of the reference does not have a direct bearing on that. However, if this is a matter of particular grievance to the client then it is important for you to take it seriously and deal with it. You may find, for example, that the client has a job interview coming up and therefore is anxious in the short-term to settle the matter of the reference.

It is also worth thinking about and discussing any possible future anxieties. The lawyer is in a better position than the client to anticipate these, since the lawyer already knows what the client's present concerns are and also has the benefit of experience in seeing how different cases affect clients. Similar circumstances affect individual clients in different ways. It is important that the lawyer is forthcoming about future events which might cause the client to worry; for example, if you already know that it will be at least a year until the trial takes place, then you should say so. At least then the client knows the situation and even if she is dismayed and disappointed at the length of the delay, she is under no false illusions about the time it might take to achieve her goals.

Another important aspect of the process of identifying client goals is to recognise your client's expectations: does your client know what she wants? Has she already made a decision and then came to you for confirmation? Or is your client hoping and expecting that you will make a decision for her?

It is not unusual, particularly for inexperienced lawyers, to think that they must solve the problem alone, because that is their job. Do remember that the client is your chief resource *and* is likely to have views about the *best possible* outcome for her - even if she finally has to settle for the *least worst* option.

## 5.7    Collaborative decision-making

Ideally, it is at this stage that a plan of action can be agreed. If necessary, you can repeat your advice on the different courses of action and their merits. The client then has the opportunity to exercise his judgment regarding the various alternatives for action, can criticise and make amendments, and finally come to an agreement with you on a course of action to be taken.

When it comes to making the final decision, you are strongly advised that this is generally best left to the client to decide on the basis of his own preference, taking into account the information and advice you have given. It seems that a client can live with the decision better if it is one that he has made personally. As his lawyer you can guide your client in the direction that you feel would best serve his interests. For example, in the earlier example, Mr Knossos stated clearly that he did not want to go to court and is prepared to have the repairs done provided he gets the rent.

What about the client who wants you to make the decision? In commercial matters the client often expects her legal adviser to understand the context of the decision sufficiently so that the lawyer is perceived as fulfilling the role of legal adviser and decision-maker. In other contexts, for example personal injury litigation, the client may have no idea of the chances of success if the case goes to trial and may prefer the lawyer to decide on a settlement. You will need to explain the system of paying into court and the risk of a costs penalty if the court's award is less than the sum paid in; the length of time to get to trial; and the reimbursement to the legal aid fund for any compensation received. If after providing these explanations the client still wants you to decide, you can only state your preferred choice but leave it to the client to adopt that as his decision.

What if the client chooses the worst possible option in your view? Imagine, for example, that your client has been found in possession of a Class A drug. He wants to plead not guilty and go to trial by jury at the crown court. He claims that the police planted the drug on him during the course of the search outside a club. There are no witnesses to the search nor any mention of it in the police statements. You explain the difficulties of his defence and, since this is a first offence, you advise that were he to plead guilty in a magistrate's court he would probably be dealt with by way of a fine and that costs would be much less. This would be so even if he were to plead not guilty in the magistrate's court. Nonetheless he wants to go ahead and plead not guilty in a jury trial. In such circumstances you must respect his choice however doubtful you think his chances of success.

What about the client who has admitted his guilt but insists on pleading not guilty? Since a solicitor is an officer of the Court, there is an apparent conflict between the duty owed to the client and the duty owed to the Court. A solicitor must not mislead the Court or withhold information to which the Court is entitled. She must not act for a client who has admitted perjury in those particular proceedings, unless this can be fully disclosed to the Court. A solicitor cannot represent a defendant who wishes to give evidence in the witness box denying guilt, or assist him in the preparation of statements claiming his innocence. However, since the prosecution is required to prove guilt, the solicitor can represent a client on this basis only and may submit that the prosecution has not discharged the burden of proof, that is, that there is insufficient evidence to justify a conviction. Clearly, if the defendant is found guilty, the solicitor cannot mitigate on the grounds that the defendant was innocent of the charge nor that he co-operated fully with the police.

## 5.8    Difficult situations

Some aspects of the advising and counselling process which lawyers find particularly difficult are discussed further below.

### 5.8.1    Giving bad news

Just as clients may tell lawyers what they think the lawyer wants to hear and are anxious to justify themselves in order to win the lawyer's support, it can be difficult for lawyers to give 'bad news'. By this I mean anything which the lawyer finds embarrassing or discomforting to say, either because of the nature of the information or because of the negative response it is likely to induce in the client; for example embarrassment, disbelief, outrage, anger or tears. Discussing money (fees and costs) may produce any or all of these reactions which is probably why lawyers sometimes find it difficult to be straightforward about fees. (See also para 5.8.5 below.)

Other areas which lawyers find difficult to discuss with their client include:

- telling him that you don't believe him
- advising her that there is no legal remedy (for example, the video camera example in Chapter One)
- advising him that he is likely to lose/be convicted
- explaining that you cannot do what the client wants on the grounds that it is unethical or even unlawful.

Although it is undeniably difficult to give bad news, it is preferable to be as clear and straightforward as you can, choosing your words tactfully and trying to adopt an objective and supportive stance. The danger of dressing-up the information to cushion the blow is that this can result in ambiguity and the client failing to understand your message. It is far better to be straightforward with the client and tell him bad news as clearly and as tactfully as you can, than to avoid telling him at all. The client will appreciate your honesty, instead of being fobbed off with vague and evasive answers.

For example, imagine that you have been sent to court to make a bail application for a client in custody. After speaking to the prosecutor and checking the file with the court clerk, you discover that at a hearing the previous week when your client was represented by the duty solicitor, your client was committed in custody for sentence on another matter to a crown court. Therefore, any bail application you make would be academic because your client would not be released in any event until he had been sentenced in the outstanding matter.

You now have to go down to the cells of the court to inform your client of this. Your client is likely to be angry and upset and you will be on the receiving end. Try not to take this personally, and to recognise why your client feels this way. Allow your client time to calm down and then suggest constructive solutions, such as attempting to have his outstanding matter for sentence listed as soon as possible. If he were to receive a non-custodial sentence, bail might then be applied for regarding the matter in hand. The client will probably still be angry - he has to remain in custody - but at least you have given him a realistic view of his position and a practical remedy for his problems. (See also Chapter Six at para 6.5.)

### 5.8.2   Distressed clients

In Chapter Four we considered how you might deal with a weeping client. Distress can be shown in other ways, not least the making of irrational decisions. In such cases you will need to counsel the client to delay making a decision until he or she feels calmer and has thought about it. You will also need to show both sympathy and empathy in order to win the client's confidence and trust.

Effective responses include:

- giving the client time to recover - don't be afraid of silence
- speaking quietly
- active listening and reflecting back are both essential
- discussing relevant matters in a calm and logical way

### 5.8.3   Angry/aggressive clients

Anger and aggression can be very intimidating and difficult to handle, whether or not you have been the cause, or simply on the receiving end (you just 'happen to be there'). Before discussing some basic tactics try and think of a situation where *you* felt angry or aggrieved. What did you do?

Generally, anger is evident because it is expressed explosively with words and/or gestures, although in some cases it is manifested by an icy calm. In the former situation, the interviewer may feel quite threatened, while in the latter the danger is that you may not recognise how angry the client is and therefore respond inappropriately, triggering off the explosion. Thinking about situations in which you have felt real anger will probably lead you to the conclusion that it was impossible to contain and you had to express it. This suggests that it is wise to let an angry client get it out of his or her system, since attempts to stem the flow may be ineffectual and merely prolong the situation.

What you do after the initial outburst? Think about how your own anger was responded to and what was done to dissipate it effectively. Was the response ineffective because the other person became angry in return, or backed off helplessly?

Having let the client express his anger, wait for an appropriate pause and, if possible, sit down and encourage the client to join you. It is important to respond positively. For example:

'I am extremely sorry that you were kept waiting for so long and that you feel you were treated rudely. I will do my best to find out what happened.'

This is a reasonably straightforward situation but the client may often be angry for a variety of reasons and not necessarily coherent in expressing them. There is a real danger that you will not discover the true facts because you want to avoid a fresh outburst by re-opening the matters that caused it originally. However, it is important to first clarify the situation:

'I appreciate that you are angry and I need to make sure of the facts so that we can sort things out.'

You should then summarise carefully what you may have discovered or, if you are unsure, ask the client to explain the sequence of events since any misunderstanding on your part may be inflammatory.

Another danger is that you may be bullied into rash promises. If you or your firm is at fault, your best bet is to be genuinely abject and try to retrieve something positive from the situation.

Extremes of emotion like anger do eventually dissipate, of course, but aggressive clients are harder to handle since there is often a continuing pattern of behaviour which can be exhausting or cause you to feel angry yourself. Bad behaviour tends to breed bad behaviour, but you will need to exercise self control to resist this response. As a last resort you may use the tactic of suggesting that the client does not seem very happy with you and would perhaps prefer to see someone else.

Calmness, patience and reasonableness are all essential but so is the ability to empathise with angry or aggressive clients, however unsympathetic or threatened you may feel.

Effective responses to angry/aggressive behaviour include:

- remaining calm and polite
- listening - be patient and don't interrupt
- avoiding eye contact (since eye contact is usually taken as encouraging behaviour, avoidance tends to discourage)
- being positive and standing your ground. The natural instinct may well be to retreat behind a barrier - a table or chair - but there is evidence (for example from the experience of those working in Department of Social Services offices) that barriers tend to make the situation worse.

### 5.8.4    Indecisive clients

When it comes to making decisions, clients may be hesitant about deciding what to do for a variety of reasons:

1  This client may find all decision-making difficult, or it may be simply that the client is unused to having to make decisions of this sort.

2  The client may not fully understand the options and consequences.

3  The options are all equally undesirable and none represent the solution the client anticipated or wanted.

4  The client's motives (for example, revenge) may be in conflict with the outcome that would be in his best interests.

Some strategies you may use to help the client decide include:

- explain and clarify the options and consequences to ensure that the client fully understands
- discuss the advantages and disadvantages of each option

- ask the client what the best and worst possible outcome may be in her view and then deal with what is possible or likely in the circumstances
- ask the client to prioritise
- give the client more time, if that is possible. You could suggest that she writes down the options, the advantages and disadvantages and so on so that you can consider them together. If there is time, you could offer to put this in writing.

If the client insists that you make the decision, it is advisable to make it clear that although you personally would choose a particular course of action, it is the client who has to live with the decision and its consequences.

### 5.8.5   Discussing fees

Most clients have little or no idea of the basis on which legal fees are calculated and will no doubt be concerned about cost, or potential cost, particularly if the matter goes to court. Clients need information about how legal fees are worked out, so that they can develop a perception of value for money. This is particularly true of business clients who will also be more confident about bargaining and negotiating a good deal.

The amount you can charge is moderated by statute and depends on whether the work is contentious or non-contentious. In both cases, however, the underlying principle to be applied is that the client must pay a fair and reasonable sum for work done on her instructions. It is therefore of paramount importance that it is clear that the client is instructing you and the nature of those instructions, that is, that there is a contract between you and the content of that contract.

Under the Solicitors' Act 1974 all work is non-contentious unless it is for the purposes of proceedings which have in fact begun, that is, by the issue of a writ or summons. This means that in some cases charges will cover both contentious and non-contentious work. The significance of the distinction is that the client is entitled to have costs for the contentious business taxed, and the amount will be at the discretion of the taxing officer in accordance with the appropriate rules of court. (RSC Ord 62, CCR Ord 38).

For non-contentious work, the Solicitors' Remuneration Order 1972 will apply. The client is entitled to require the solicitor to obtain a certificate from the Law Society stating that the sum charged is 'fair and reasonable'. The relevant considerations for what is fair and reasonable include the complexity or difficulty of the matter, the time spent, the skill, specialist knowledge, responsibility and documentation involved, the value of the subject matter and importance to the client. These costs belong to the solicitor, whereas costs awarded to the successful litigant belong to her. Clearly it is the lawyer's duty to warn the client that if unsuccessful, she will be liable to pay the other party's costs.

If you consider for a moment how a solicitor's bill is calculated, you will realise that the cost to the client must take into account not only the statutory controls but how much time has been spent on the job and how much that time has cost the firm. For this reason it is usual for solicitors to keep time sheets and record by way of attendance notes and the like, the actual amount of time spent on a matter. This is of particular importance if the bill is sent to the taxing officer or Law Society for scrutiny.

You will often be unable to give an accurate estimate of cost to a client and in any event need to be cautious on this score since you may later be held to that sum even if the matter costs a great deal more. However you should at least explain how your fees will be calculated and whether that includes VAT and disbursements, for example stamp duty. (See Rule 15(1) Professional Code of Conduct of Solicitors 1993, Appendix A, Chapter One.)

The client is entitled to put a limit on the costs and to ask for a regular report. Equally, you are entitled to ask for interim payments as the matter proceeds and even for a sum of money 'up front'. You should of course both consider whether the matter is justified by the likely costs and chance of success, particularly in contentious matters.

Two other points you should always consider in relation to costs are whether the fees may be covered by insurance and whether the client is entitled to legal aid. If your client is entitled to legal aid you should outline how the scheme works, explaining the income limits and any contributions your client may have to make. The following points need to be brought to the client's attention:

- the effect of the statutory charge
- the consequences of the other side being legally aided in relation to contribution to your costs, should you win
- that the client may have to pay the other party's costs or a contribution towards them if the case is lost, even if she is legally aided for her own costs.

In relation to criminal legal aid, you should explain in straightforward terms whether the client is likely to get legal aid and make the appropriate application. You should however warn the client that he may be ordered by the court to pay a contribution towards the costs even though legally aided.

## 5.9    Ending the interview

Leave enough time towards the end of the interview for the client to ask any further questions. Although this will probably be a formality in most cases since hopefully you will have managed to deal with all the client's queries already, it is important for the client to be given the chance of a final say. Ask, 'do you have any further questions?' in such a way that the client does not feel that you are longing to finish the interview; for example, do not start tidying your papers and looking at your watch, but be genuine about giving your client a last opportunity (in this interview) to ask questions.

Make sure that the client is absolutely clear about any plan of action and what will happen next, including any follow-up work to be done by both you and the client. Give some idea of the time scale of events if possible and arrange the next contact whether by telephone, letter or meeting. End the interview positively to avoid 'hovering', action-replays of parts of the interview and similar behaviour which may leave the client uncertain as to whether or not the interview has ended.

## 5.10 Summary

- make sure you have all the available information, including both facts and feelings
- identify the client's goals
- explain options and consequences
- offer advice non-judgmentally and without directing the client to a particular decision
- involve the client in decision-making
- assist and support the client's decision
- make sure the client knows what is likely to happen next

# Appendix

## F Clear explanations: Feedback and Commentary

1 Questions for the speaker

- What did you find difficult about this exercise?
- What made you aware of whether or not your audience was following your explanation?
- If you were aware, how did your respond?
- What assumptions did you make about the level of knowledge of your audience?
- Were you able to identify and explain jargon?

2 Questions for the listener

- How well did you understand the explanation?
- What strategies did the speaker use to promote understanding; for example, analogy, gestures and mime, visual aids - drawing diagrams etc
- What jargon was used? Was it recognised and explained and if so, how?
- How responsive was the speaker to his/her audience?
- How did the speaker demonstrate responsiveness to the audience?
- What got in the way of listening?

## Commentary

This exercise should illustrate how easy it is to take jargon for granted and therefore to be unaware of its use. Even if the listener does not interrupt with questions, it should be possible for the speaker to be aware of the response. People show understanding by nodding just as they show confusion by perhaps frowning or looking puzzled or uncertain. Recognising jargon is one thing, explaining it clearly is another. Useful strategies are to use an analogy with something with which the audience is familiar. For example, you might explain that a lease gives you rights over property for a certain period of time, similar to that of an owner, while a licence is more comparable with staying in a hotel as a guest.

In a legal context, the use of visual aids such as diagrams and flow-charts can be particularly useful to the client in working out and explaining complex relationships, for example, matters involving a number of company subsidiaries, or in landlord and tenant problems where there have been a series of underleases.

As the listener you may have found that thinking about what you were going to say affected your concentration (see para 4.2 'Active listening'). Alternatively, if you are listening, having already done the exercise, you may be reviewing your own performance, and making comparisons instead of listening.

The feedback you give and receive from each other (see Chapter Six) is an essential part of the exercise. However, make sure that you wait until you have all completed your explanations before offering comments on your own and your colleagues' performance.

# CHAPTER

## 6  Reflection and Evaluation

'*Experience is the name everyone gives to their mistakes.*'

Oscar Wilde
(Lady Windermere's Fan)

## 6.1     Learning from experience

In order to learn from experience and develop your skills, it is necessary to reflect on that experience: how did you feel before, during and after the interview? What was good and bad about the interview? What did you learn about yourself? What are your strengths and weaknesses? How can you build on the strengths and improve on the weaknesses?

You should already have developed the habit of reviewing your own communication skills in a variety of situations (see Chapter Two). Initially, we often do this in a rather vague way:

'I felt that the interview went well/badly'.

The next stage is to examine and assess the evidence you may have to support this feeling or belief. After reflection, analysis and evaluation the final stage is to develop strategies that will help you to absorb and gain from your learned experience.

Once you are aware of the elements of effective interviewing, you should be able to apply the process of analysis and evaluation to any interviews you observe whether in practice, on television or which you might hear on the radio. Although the objectives may be different in each interview the principles are the same. Consider first in each case what the objectives might be or what you think the interview was trying to achieve (for example, to gain information, a PR or promotion exercise or to score points). Then consider how effective the interviewer was and what techniques were used. A great deal may be learned from watching and listening to experienced interviewers, including when they get it wrong. For example, on some occasions a politician might become so incensed that the interview becomes a series of interruptions or breaks down altogether. That may well have been the interviewer's intention because it makes for a more exciting broadcast but it is not an effective interview!

In Chapter Two you were asked to analyse elements of a 'bad' interview which you had experienced and various criteria were suggested for assessing effective interviews. The expressions 'good' and 'bad' are often criticised as subjective and based on personal preferences. This problem can be minimised by providing clear criteria to focus on effectiveness rather than personal likes and dislikes. We are all capable of making judgments about whether a particular performance is good or bad; for example, in the arts, architecture, the performing arts, sports and professionally. However this is often confused with how we feel about the thing itself or about the performer so that 'good' tends to equal 'like', and 'bad' what we 'dislike'.

It requires a particular discipline to be a critic and to divorce our subjective feelings as far as possible from the application of objective criteria. Fortunately this is not really necessary in our personal predilections. We can like whatever music, art and so on that appeals to us and be prepared to explain why. When it comes to assessing the demonstration of communication skills, it is extremely important to keep separate as far as possible the effectiveness of the performance (which can be measured against objective criteria) from our personal views about the style and personality of the performer. Individuals can develop their practical skills, but they cannot be asked to change their personalities in a radical way. Nevertheless it is also true that developing skills helps to build personal confidence - the diffident may become more assertive for example - and experience encourages self-awareness.

Reflection, analysis and assessment in reviewing an interview can be seen from three different perspectives:

- the interviewer
- the client
- the observer

We will consider these in turn as the basis for review and evaluation.

## 6.2    The interviewer's perspective

### 6.2.1    First impressions

It has been stressed throughout this book that how clients themselves feel and perceive their problems and concerns is of great relevance to the lawyer. It is equally true that your own feelings and perceptions about the client and the interview are important.

Begin by asking yourself the question 'How would you evaluate the interview generally?' In other words, how did you feel about it? You may want to award marks out of ten or mentally tick boxes 'very good', 'good', 'satisfactory', 'poor' or award A, B+, B, C. Use whatever grading system suits you. Note that you are not awarding grades merely for your own performance but for the whole process. An interview may *feel* 'very good' because, for example, the client was pleasant and co-operative and you felt relaxed and confident. Alternatively, the interview might have been difficult for a number of reasons, not least that you disliked the person you were interviewing. It may seem obvious to point out that you will occasionally meet clients with whom you find it difficult to empathise; for example clients who are irritating, arrogant, boring, or complain a lot. Meetings with such people are unlikely to *feel* 'very good' and will therefore probably attract a low score, when in reality and on closer analysis they may in fact have been effective and competent interviews. The overall impression of the interview is therefore a good starting point for evaluation, but your reflection should not end there if you are really going to learn from the experience.

### 6.2.2   Analysis

Having awarded the interview an overall score, make a brief note of why you think it was good or bad. Indicators may include the following:

- the client's demeanour throughout the interview but particularly at the start. Did the nervous, worried, or hostile client become more relaxed? If the client's demeanour deteriorated during the course of the interview was this because of the bad news you had to give or because of the way you were managing the interview. (Be honest with yourself.)

- how much information was volunteered? Did you feel you had to quarry for it or, alternatively that you were unable to stem the flow?

- did the client ask a lot of questions? This may mean that your explanation and advice was not clear or that you asked too many closed questions. Closed questions towards or at the end of the interview may also indicate that you probably talked too much, and did not give the client sufficient opportunity during the information-gathering stage to discuss matters of importance to him/her.

- consider your questioning style generally. Was there an appropriate blend of open and closed questions?

- assess your use of language and particularly jargon when giving advice and information.

- what impression do you think you made? For example, if you were feeling tired or preoccupied did that appear to interfere with your concentration? Did the client have to tell you the same thing more than once? Was it apparent that you were having difficulty in following the client's story?

- consider your body language. Did you show empathy/ antipathy? Disapproval? Were you at any point judgmental?

- finally, consider the quality of your notes. It is essential to dictate or write them up more fully while details are fresh in your mind.

Memory cannot be relied upon and it is not advisable to write verbatim notes while you are interviewing since you will not be able to concentrate on listening and observing.

Your notes may well reveal gaps, inconsistencies, uncertainties and omissions. Did your attention stray? Was your questioning and probing inadequate? Did you forget to cover a particular point? If necessary, a follow-up telephone call or letter may be necessary to clarify matters but this should be done quickly while the interview is still fresh in the client's mind also.

## 6.3    The client's perspective

In the process of close analysis, it will help to try and put yourself in the client's shoes and consider how he or she would have scored the interview, and why? This involves repeating the process, which is described above, from the client's perspective. It requires you to step outside yourself and consider how you appeared and behaved, rather than how you felt you appeared and behaved.

### 6.3.1    Learning through role-play

A very useful technique to help you develop this objective approach is to play the part of the client in role-play, as well as participating as an interviewer or an observer. Role-play can be of enormous benefit, particularly if it is possible to video the interview for discussion and feedback afterwards. Even without video, it is extremely useful to compare the views and observations of the role-play participants.

Firstly, role-play provides experience which simulates a real life situation as closely as possible. This helps to accelerate learning in a structured format and provides practice in behaviour. For example, it helps you to train yourself to control your emotions. These experiences can also change behaviour and attitudes.

Secondly, role-play provides the opportunity for feedback from the client and any observer(s). This gives you two perspectives which do not always coincide, since the client's viewpoint is highly subjective: what did it feel like to be interviewed? The observer's viewpoint can be more objective: how did the interview process appear, measured against agreed criteria? The client's view reflects personal feelings about how he or she was treated as a client and whether he or she would trust and have confidence in that interviewer. The observer's assessment can be based only on how this is translated into observable behaviour, together with how well the interview has achieved its purpose. It is helpful for the observer to have written criteria and to make notes during the interview. Suggested assessment criteria can be found in Appendix F in the form of a checklist which can be completed by interviewer, observer and client and then compared and discussed.

In real life, of course, the only reviewer is likely to be you, the 'interviewer'. The client may rarely voice an opinion and you will seldom have the benefit of an observer to provide feedback. For this reason it is particularly helpful to use role-play during your training since it gives you the opportunity to learn on the job, to make mistakes in a safe situation and to review your performance with the help of others. This accelerates learning and helps to build confidence.

Careful preparation is needed for role-plays to be successful. To get the most from the experience as a client and to assist the colleague(s) who are interviewing you, it is important to prepare for your role carefully, thinking yourself into the client's persona. This includes taking on the persona of the client in relation to knowledge of the law, so that if, for example, the interviewer uses legal jargon you should be able to react - 'what does that mean?' - as the client would. It is important to be as plausible as possible and avoid the temptation to over-act.

By thinking yourself into the client's role you have a unique opportunity to feel what it is like to be on the receiving end of a lawyer/client interview. Try to make a mental note of observations and comments you can usefully contribute to the post-interview review. Do remember to be positive and present your criticisms as constructively as possible. (See also para 6.6 below.)

A number of role-play scenarios are provided for your use in Chapter Seven.

## 6.4    The observer's role

The same principles apply if you are observing a role-play interview. It is helpful to have a list of criteria and to use this as the basis of your review. A checklist (Appendix G at the end of this chapter) is appended together with the judging criteria used in the Client Interviewing Competition. These have been adapted from the International Client Counselling Competition and have therefore been tried and tested over a considerable number of years. It is suggested that in your observations you try to cover the following areas:

- The lawyer/client relationship

  This will include issues of confidentiality, fees and costs, conflict of interests as well as the establishing of the professional relationship and how the client was treated generally from hello, to goodbye.

- Information gathering

  Including evidence of listening, questioning (note the effectiveness of the types of questions used), time management and summarising the information accurately.

- Advising and counselling

  Including:

    - clarity and accuracy of advice including a description of the consequences/implications of various options

    - awareness of the client's needs and preferences based on an understanding of their situation, business interests etc.

    - both legal and non-legal options for example, self-help or recourse to other agencies (but do ask the client what he/she wants to do)

    - dealing with moral and ethical issues

    - involving the client in the decision-making process.

## 6.5    Exercise: Giving feedback

In Chapter Five we considered the problem of giving bad news
(para 5.8.1). For example, it may seem damaging to the
relationship of trust to have to say to a client 'I don't think you are
being completely honest with me' since in effect you are saying 'I
think you are lying'. It is therefore much easier to let the client off
the hook and accept what you are told. However there are ways of
saying this and giving other 'bad news' which can be positive and
not destroy the relationship. For example, you may say to a client
whom you suspect of non-disclosure or of lying:

> 'There are things here that don't quite add up. Perhaps we could
> go through the facts again since it is really important for me to
> know everything in order to advise you and represent you properly.'

The skill dimension in giving bad news lies in how you present
it. The straight negative with the explanation that the law may work
unjustly or harshly in your client's case but 'that's the law, I'm afraid'
will be small comfort. The same would be the case if you presented
feedback to your fellow students or colleagues in this manner. If the
bad news is presented as part of a package which contains some
positive suggestions then lawyer and client may be able to work
towards the best possible alternative solution. Obviously there will
be situations which are beyond redemption but even these can be
mitigated in the presentation:

> 'I think you know already that this means you will be sent inside,
> but I will do my best to argue for the shortest possible time. You will
> be pleading guilty and you have co-operated with the police which
> all helps. Can we get a letter from your employer to say he will
> keep your job open for you?' etc.

A useful way of practising your presentation of giving bad news
and at the same time assisting colleagues is in giving feedback if
you are acting as a client or observing colleagues interviewing. It is
essential that you are honest and some of your comments may be
negative - in other words, bad news. Since nobody likes to receive
criticism, this part of your feedback may be muffled in vagueness. It
would be much more useful, however, if it was clear and specific.

For this exercise, try to think of some positive ways of presenting feedback which is specific and constructive in the following situations:

- where the interviewer was judgmental and patronising
- where the interviewer failed to obtain accurate information by not testing it
- where the interviewer failed to obtain accurate information and to give relevant advice because he/she did not focus on the issues but allowed the client to ramble
- where the advice given was falsely optimistic because the interviewer did not want to give bad news
- where the advice given failed to take into account the client's needs and focused only on the legal solutions
- where the client failed to understand the advice given

Developing the skill of giving bad news will be useful to you in many situations. Giving criticism in a constructive and useful form is a valuable skill which is also relevant in other aspects of lawyering including, for example, the supervision of junior staff and management of secretaries and support staff.

## 6.6     Guidelines for giving feedback

- always start with positive comments
- praise generously the elements that were good about the interview
- encourage the interviewer to review his/her own performance before adding your own comments
- make negative or adverse comments with care, for example, 'Perhaps you could improve eye contact if you reduce the note-taking': 'I think you may have given the impression that you were taking over from the client'
- criticise behaviour not the person and keep the two separate.

Compare for example the previous comment with this 'Well, you were rather aggressive with the client'

• be specific and give examples of the interviewer's behaviour (good and bad)

• be clear and unambiguous: vague comments do not help the learning process.

Practice in giving structured feedback both from the observer's and the client's point of view should enable you to develop a checklist with which to review and evaluate your own performance critically and honestly after every interview. This is a useful habit which will help you to continue to develop skills and avoid complacency or the adoption of a 'formula' approach. Some possible outlines for checklists of criteria which can be used as a basis for feedback on an interview are provided in Appendix G to this chapter.

Getting it wrong can be a valuable learning experience if you analyse and understand why. So do not be discouraged when things sometimes go less well than you had hoped but turn this to your positive advantage.

## 6.7    Receiving feedback

Not everyone will be expert in giving you suitably phrased constructive criticism about your performance. However, it is equally important to be able to receive feedback in a positive way to help you to learn and improve your interviewing skills. You will learn more about how to give and receive feedback from being on the receiving end. Giving and receiving feedback should always be a dialogue and you should avoid at all costs turning it into an argument.

The following is a list of do's and dont's to help you to accept criticism, even from those who are not skilled at presenting their comments constructively and usefully.

Do:

- be open minded and relaxed
- be responsive
- ask for specific examples
- be rational and able to accept that you may have been wrong however justified you feel
- be positive.

If at all possible, don't:

- take comments personally (ie separate *yourself* from your *performance*)
- be defensive
- be opinionated
- be over-sensitive
- let the criticism damage your confidence.

# Appendix

 Guidelines for giving feedback

## 1    Observers checklist

*The following checklist has been used in a number of professional skills training workshops for giving immediate feedback.*

While you are observing the interview it may be helpful to consider the following points and grade from 5 - 0 where 5 = excellent, 4 = very good, 3 = good, 2 = needs improvement, 1 = poor, 0 = very poor.

Please add comments where appropriate. Do remember to start with positive feedback and present adverse comments tactfully.

1   **How did you rate the interview overall?**                     [ ]

2   **Establishing rapport:**         **overall grade**            [ ]

Meeting and greeting                                              [ ]

Eye contact                                                       [ ]

Non-verbal communication                                          [ ]

Empathy/responsiveness                                            [ ]

**3  Information gathering:**        **overall grade**                [ ]

   Listening skills                                                   [ ]


   Accurate summary of facts                                          [ ]


   Questioning skills                                                 [ ]
   (Appropriate use of open and closed
   questions, avoidance of leading questions)


**4  Advice and explanation:**        **overall grade**               [ ]

   Understanding client's needs/wants                                 [ ]


   Use of appropriate language                                        [ ]
   (eg avoidance of jargon)


   Clarity                                                            [ ]


**5  Suggested areas for improvement:**

## 2    Client Interviewing Competition

### (i)    Judge's comment sheet

*The following judge's comment sheet was adapted by Martin Davis of the Client Interviewing Committee from guidelines provided by the International Client Counselling Competition.*

It is suggested that a five point scale is used for marking the four elements of the interview with each element being graded A, B, C, D, or E as appropriate. The final grade/mark for each team will, therefore, result from the combination of grades given for the individual elements.

A = Excellent

B = Good

C = Satisfactory

D = Less than satisfactory

E = Poor

## (ii)    Client Interviewing Competition:
         Standards for judging

## A    General

1    One of the main differences between the Client Interviewing
     Competition and the majority of other Law School competitive
     formats is that the students face a person rather than merely a
     problem. Judges should bear this fundamental point in mind
     throughout, and should be particularly critical of teams which
     inflexibly adopt preset formulas rather than respond to the
     person in front of them.

2    Another distinctive feature of the competition is the emphasis it
     places on teamwork rather than individual performance.
     Judges should take careful note of how well the interviewers
     collaborate and work as a team - rather than as two individuals
     who happen to be interviewing the client together!

3    A third, important (if less tangible) general point is the overall
     'atmosphere' of the interviews. Clearly there is no 'ideal'
     atmosphere - it all depends on the complex interaction of
     lawyers and client. However, as the interview develops it
     should become clear whether the overall atmosphere is one of
     sympathetic cooperation and mutual trust and confidence or
     (at the other extreme) one of guardedness and mutual hostility!

     The remaining comments on standards should be read
in conjunction with the judge's comment sheets to which they
cross relate.

## Element 1: General atmosphere/relationship with the client

1 Have the lawyers taken steps to establish a satisfactory professional relationship with the client?

**Comments:**

2 Were the lawyers able to deal with the client's emotional problems?

**Comments:**

3 Was the issue of costs/fees dealt with satisfactorily?

**Comments:**

Grade (A - E)

## Element II: Collection of information/fact gathering

1   Have the lawyers obtained all relevant information, from the
    client, concerning the client's problem, that is necessary for the
    interview to proceed fruitfully?
    **Comments:**

2   Did the lawyers use the available time efficiently and
    coherently? Did they display an ability to move between
    questioning (open and closed) and listening to respond to the
    needs of the particular client, and the particular case?
    **Comments:**

3   Have the lawyers reflected back to the client an accurate
    understanding of the problem?
    **Comments:**

Grade (A - E)

## Element III: Advice giving

1  Were the lawyers able to handle moral and ethical issues raised by the client and his/her problem

   **Comments:**

2  Have the lawyers clearly indicated the options for action, both legal and non-legal, and explained the consequences and allowed or assisted the client to choose a course(s) of action?

   **Comments:**

3  Once a course of action was adopted did the lawyers outline a clear campaign? Was it clear what the lawyers would do and what the client had to do?

   **Comments:**

4  Did the client appear to be reassured? Had immediate problems been dealt with?

   **Comments:**

Grade (A - E)

## Element IV: Post interview reflection

Did the lawyers use their time fully and profitably, both reflecting on the interview itself and considering future strategies?

Grade (A - E)

—-0—-

**Final grades:**

**ELEMENT I**     **ELEMENT II**     **ELEMENT III**     **ELEMENT IV**

A = 5
B = 4
C = 3
D = 2
E = 1

Overall mark:

## B  Element I: General atmosphere/relationship with the client

1.1  Did the lawyers attempt to explain their professional role, and how, in general terms, they might hope to work with the client to help resolve his-her problems?

1.2  Did the lawyers attempt to explain to the client the professional constraints and standards under which they operated? If this was explained, did the lawyers show concern for the client's understanding of the 'rules' under which lawyers work or were these 'rules' merely proclaimed?

2.1  Did the lawyers appear to take note of the client's initial feelings and attitudes?

2.2  Did the lawyers reflect back to the client their awareness of, and concern with his/her situation in a sympathetic manner?

3.1  Was the issue of fees resolved in such a way that the client understood the likely costs involved?

3.2  When the issue of fees was raised by the lawyers, was its appearance timely?

3.3  Did the raising of the issue of fees seem to threaten the client? If so, how was this dealt with (Note: all participants have been supplied with a uniform fee schedule, a copy of which is contained in the competition rules).

## C   Element 2: Collection of information/fact gathering

In most preliminary interviews, the first item on the professional
agenda is for the salient facts to be established. Most research on
interviewing and counselling suggests that (aside from other
considerations) the facts are established most effectively when the
client is encouraged to talk freely, and the lawyer appears to be
listening! Lawyers 'prompts' via 'open' questions likeliest to facilitate
this process, rather than a cross-examination style. There will,
however, be situations - perhaps with a very 'reluctant' or
(conversely) a very hostile client where other approaches are
required. Again, flexibility is the key.

1.1  Did the lawyers obtain all salient information from the client,
     concerning the client's problem? (As judges you will have
     exactly the same 'brief' as the actor/client is working from.)

1.2  Did this 'fact gathering' result in a clear formulation of the
     client's problem(s)?

1.3  Did the lawyers 'rush to judgment' before they had established
     all the relevant facts?

2.1  Did the lawyers appear to proceed in a logical manner in their
     framing of successive questions.

2.2  Equally, did the lawyers demonstrate the capacity to learn from
     the client, and show that they could abandon a preset line of
     questioning if it appeared fruitless?

2.3  Was the use of questioning styles - open or closed - appropriate
     to the situation, and the client?

2.4  Did the lawyers listen to the client, and indicate that they
     understood the problem from the client's perspective?

## D   Element 3: Advice giving

Most commentators suggest that the lawyer-client relationship works best when it is collaborative, and that the client is usually more satisfied with his/her lawyer (and more likely to follow advice!) when he/she has (at least) had a hand in the proposed 'solutions'. Of course, situations and clients vary - some clients will look to the lawyer for 'solutions' - others will instinctively see it as their case, in the resolution of which the lawyer is a partner.

1.1 In addition to the general awareness displayed of the client's needs, how did the lawyers handle (any) more/ethical issues raised by the client and his/her problem?

1.2 Did the lawyers appear to 'fight shy' of dealing with such issues, or were they able to (at least) articulate the problem(s) and begin to grapple with it/them?

2.1 Did the lawyers explain the relevant law in a clear manner, and at an appropriate point in the interview?

2.2 Were the lawyers able to articulate possible solutions to the client's problem(s), and to indicate the pros and cons of alternative strategies?

2.3 In so far as 'non legal' matters presented themselves (emotional conflicts moral issues/financial matters etc) were the lawyers able to clearly link them to the legal issue for the client's benefit, and did they acknowledge any responsibility for offering advice on such matters.

2.4 In the formulation of a strategy for resolving the client's problem - did the client appear to feel free to ask questions; challenge suggestions; and offer his/her own thoughts. Indeed, was the client encouraged to do so?

3.1 Did the client appear to understand the proposed course(s) of action - legal and non-legal?

3.2 Did the lawyers make it clear what they would be doing, and what the client should be doing?

3.3 Was an attempt made to indicate the likely timescale involved?

4.1 Did the lawyers manage to identify any immediate problems which required 'fire brigade' treatment, in addition to longer term strategies?

4.2 Did the client appear to be informed and (where appropriate) reassured? - (judges may choose to cross-check this with the client between interviews).

## E    Element 4: Post-interview reflection

It is important that the lawyers take this part of the competition seriously. It provides an important opportunity for them to reflect on the interview; identify gaps in the information they have acquired; and flush out further strategies/tactics. Any *questions to the lawyers from the judges should only arise when it is clear that they have finished their discussion.*

Amongst the points that could arise at this stage are:

1    Did the lawyers notice what they had omitted to do, or to discover?

2    Did the lawyers reflect on what might have been handled differently? (And what they think went well!)

3    Did the lawyers establish an agenda for what they needed to research, and for the steps they needed to take?

4    Did they talk about their own feelings towards the case (and the client), and attempt to consider further any professional/ethical dilemmas?

5    Did they reflect on how the client *appeared to* think about them?

### (iii)      More about the Client Interviewing Competition

This competition for undergraduate law students was introduced
into the United Kingdom in 1984, from North America. The
competition centres on a simulated law office interview. The
students, working in teams of two, are required to interview, and
advise, a 'client'. Their management of the interview is judged
according to agreed criteria, which include: the degree to which a
good working relationship with the client was established; how well
the legal problems were identified and handled; how sensitively
ethical and personal issues including costs were addressed; and
the appropriateness of the advice given. An additional element is
the post-interview reflection which encourages evaluation of their
own performance and provides the opportunity to identify omissions
and plan what action needs to be taken. The competition requires
students not merely to know the relevant law, but also to employ
effective interviewing techniques, and be aware of a variety of
considerations which they might not otherwise be exposed to as
law students.

In choosing a team to enter the competition, the most common
approach is via an internal competition in the individual law school.
However, selection procedures are, ultimately, for each competing
school to determine for itself.

The usual format for the competition is for all competing teams
to meet over a single weekend, hosted by the winners of the
previous year's competition. There are two heats, the finalists being
those three (or perhaps four) teams with the highest aggregate
score. For the heats, teams are randomly divided into groups of
three or four. The same problem is presented to all competing
teams, but each group has its own 'client', and panel of three judges
(a practitioner, an academic and a counsellor). Consistency
between the teams of judges is promoted by a thorough and
uniform briefing beforehand, and by agreed judging criteria and
marking systems. 'Clients' are also briefed in advance to endeavour
to achieve as much consistency as possible in the presentation of
the role. For the second heat, the teams are regrouped with different

judges, and a new 'client' with a new problem. Each interview lasts for 30 minutes with a 10 minute post-interview session.

The winners of the competition go on to compete in the International Client Counselling Competition with the winning teams from similar internal competitions in the USA., Canada, Australia and Scotland.

# CHAPTER

## 7 Role-plays

As we saw in the previous chapter, participating in role-plays is an excellent way of developing and improving the practical skills needed for interviewing and counselling. Learning takes place through the experience itself. Equally if not more importantly learning is enhanced by the process of evaluation and reflection. This means making a conscious effort to absorb and implement in practice what you have learned through that experience.

To assist you, some sample role-plays are contained in the following pages. It is valuable to take it in turns to be interviewer, client and observer, preferably in different role-plays. When you are the interviewer, resist the temptation to read the relevant facts beforehand so that you can have a realistic experience of the information gathering process. As the client, you will need to be familiar with the facts of the role-play and be as plausible as possible. You should try to be faithful to the facts you are given but don't be afraid to improvise - realistically - if you are asked a question during the interview which falls outside your given facts. The observer should also know the role-play facts and note comments briefly on an evaluation sheet (see the examples in Chapter Six).

You can practice these role-plays without an observer, but in every case the feedback session is essential, so do not omit it. At the end of the interview, the interviewer should first read the role-play facts and then assess her own performance before receiving feedback from the client and the observer.

## 7.1 How to use the role-plays

1 The interviewer reads the office memorandum for the selected role-play. Do **not** read the role-play facts until after the interview.

2 The client reads the role-play facts. Do not change the basic facts but decide how you will play the character and be as realistic as possible.

3   The observer reads both the role-play facts and the office memorandum. The observer should also study the evaluation sheet or observer's checklist, which you should select in advance and have ready for the interview.

4   Allow 30 minutes for the interview and at least 10 minutes for the feedback session.

5   The interviewer reads the role-play facts and the commentary after the interview and makes an assessment of his or her own performance.

6   The client and the observer give feedback to the interviewer based (in the case of the observer) on the evaluation sheet or observer's checklist. Remember to be constructive and supportive (see Chapter Six on giving feedback).

The commentary after each role-play provides some guidelines for points that may arise. It is not of course intended to be exhaustive because 'clients' will present the problem in different ways. Do remember that it is the interviewing skills that are being assessed, not knowledge of the law. In each case this is a *first interview* so that your advice as far as the law is concerned will not be final; you will have the opportunity to do some research before the next meeting or letter of advice. However, the client will of course expect some initial advice and information about what action will be taken.

## 7.2    Role-play 1

**Office memorandum for the interviewer**

Francis/Frances Jenkins was told by the magistrates to see a solicitor. He/she has been charged with criminal damage and has to go back to court in two weeks' time.

**Client role-play 1**

You are Francis/Frances Jenkins and have been advised by the magistrates to see a solicitor. You appeared in the local Magistrates' Court last week on a charge of criminal damage to a police car, and have been bailed to appear again in two weeks' time.

Please give your own age, address and phone number.

Your boy/girlfriend - referred to as 'partner' for convenience - is Mark/Maria Ford.

You work in a supermarket and your take-home pay is £90 per week. You give your mum £30 per week for your keep and you have no savings. Your partner lives with you in your mother's house but you don't volunteer this information - in fact you don't reveal the true facts at all unless pressed. For example, if asked, you will say that you have not been in trouble with the police before when in fact you have a conviction for shoplifting when you were 15.

The facts that you do explain are as follows:

One night a few weeks ago you were at a club with your partner and a group of friends. As you were leaving there was a fight going on outside the club, you thought 'between some black kids and some white kids'. The next thing you knew you were being bundled into a police car. You were very upset and angry and started kicking at the window of the police car from the inside and it shattered. You felt that you were 'picked on', since no-one else was arrested as far as you know. You will insist that although you had had a few drinks you were not drunk.

You told the court you wanted to plead not guilty because you didn't mean to break the window, it just happened during the struggle (you were wearing your Doc Martens at the time).

You will say at first that you did not know any of the people outside the club, but later may admit that you shouted 'fuck off' or something like that. If the solicitor probes, you will eventually admit that you have also been charged with assault but you haven't got the papers with you - you left them in your other jacket pocket. You will say that you were attacked and were defending yourself.

The true facts are that you assaulted your partner's ex-partner (Pete/Pauline Wilkins) who was also at the club (he/she is black but you see no significance in this - this is a dispute which, in your view, is not affected by race but motivated only by personal jealousy). You saw your partner and Pete/Pauline talking at one point during the evening and felt sure they were arranging to meet. You do not have a secure relationship with your partner whom you have known for about nine months, and feel miserable and jealous but find it very difficult to discuss your feelings with him/her. When you got outside the club you told Pete/Pauline to keep away from your partner, he/she replied in abusive terms and you pushed him/her. He/she fell to the ground and you kicked him/her a couple of times. You don't think the injuries were at all serious. The incident was over in minutes and you think the police just happened to be there.

You are more concerned about the deteriorating effect this incident has had on your relationship with your partner than about the court appearance. He/she would not want to be a witness. Although you say you were provoked and were defending yourself, you would be willing to plead guilty, depending on what the solicitor advises.

This is a difficult role-play in which to maintain consistency, since the amount of true information you reveal will depend to a large extent on the questioning skills of the interviewer and how the interview is handled. If you are not probed or pressed you should not volunteer the true facts. However you will have to judge whether the character you are playing would respond truthfully to the attitude or line of questioning of the solicitor. Although you want some help you are a fairly plausible liar, so that the interviewer will need to work at getting the truth from you. The character may also use a fair amount of bad language and generally present a tough kind of image but is in reality insecure. Whether or not you want the solicitor to represent you at your court appearance will depend on how you feel about him/her.

## Commentary for role-play 1

1   The client has been charged with assault and criminal damage but is only prepared to reveal the latter initially, since it touches on less sensiitive areas.

2   The main feature of this interview is the unco-operative client who is willing to reveal all the facts. This will mean that the interviewer has to test the information and be prepared to persist with a line of questioning.

3   The client does not consider this to be a racial issue although the victim is black, but the interviewer may be side-tracked into thinking it is, particularly if the client is reluctant to reveal his/her feelings.

4   A further problem is the plea. The client may be willing to plead guilty to the assault but not guilty to the criminal damage. This could be difficult in view of the attitude of the witness.

5   The question of legal aid should also be addressed.

## 7.3     Role-play 2

**Office memorandum for interviewer**

A Mrs/Mr Hampden wants to see you about a problem she/he is having with the building society. I couldn't get any more information because apparently it is 'rather complicated'.

### Client role-play 2

Name:   Mr and Mrs Hampden (please use your own address and
        telephone number).

Note:   The appointment was made by one of you so the solicitor
        will not be expecting a couple.

You will explain that you recently obtained a mortgage of £55,000
from the local branch of the Hebdon Building Society, and have
now discovered that you are being investigated for fraud.

You met and married about 10 years ago and bought your
present house. You were both working for the Priory Group, selling
life assurance and 'packaging' mortgages placed with the Hebdon
and other building societies. If asked to explain packaging, this
means obtaining employer references, valuations and doing credit
and electoral roll searches on behalf of lenders. In 1990 you came
into some money and each set up on your own - Mr H as an
independent insurance broker and Mrs H with a small catering
business called 'Hampers' (catering for weddings, parties etc)
using part-time help. Your joint annual income is around £35,000
but it is hard to assess and does fluctuate. You have hire purchase
and credit card debts of £3,000-£4,000 and no savings.

Since house prices have been falling you thought it would be a
good idea to buy another property as an investment. The idea is
that you will let the house to students and the rent will cover the
mortgage payments. When house prices rise again you can sell at
a profit. You did this before - buying a property in 1986 and selling in
1990 - and made enough money to set up on your own.

Mr H has always had a good relationship with the building
society since he places mortgages for clients with them on
occasion. However, because you know the system, you know that
your own credit rating is not good and therefore applied for this
mortgage under an assumed name. Although Mrs H knew about
the application, she did not know the details since Mr H has
handled this transaction on his own. You prepared and submitted
the package using the name of an ex-client with a good credit

rating. You prepared an employer's reference on your wife's headed paper and obtained a cheque from the building society four weeks' ago. Unfortunately for you, the person whose name you used (Martin Fairgood) applied for a mortgage himself and was refused 'because he had just been granted one through you'. Mr Fairgood phoned you to find out what was going on and you said that the building society had either confused him with someone else or there is another person of the same name.

On the previous occasion, in 1986, you bought a property as an investment, you raised the mortgage in your wife's maiden name and wrote the employer's reference bumping up her salary from £15,000 to £25,000 in order to get the sum you needed. You used licensed conveyancers for both these transactions, rather than a solicitor, because 'they are cheaper'.

The characters do not think they have done anything wrong, let alone criminal. Use phrases like 'it happens all the time, lots of people do this and some just make off with the cheques - at least we were bona fide buyers'; 'what harm have we done to anyone, we actually provide student housing and there is a need for that'. They agree that they haven't been completely honest but argue that is because building societies make it so difficult to get a mortgage if you are. If the solicitor points out that the previous application was also fraudulent you will want to explore the extent of the confidentiality undertaking so that this does not come out in the current investigation.

You understand that the building society has put the matter in the hands of the police and want to know what your legal position is regarding the alleged fraud. If the solicitor mentions tax implications, just say that your accountant deals with all that.

Mrs H may become tearful and distressed when she realises what her husband has done.

## Commentary for role-play 2

The legal issue here is mortgage fraud but the problems for the interviewer are:

1 dealing with two clients particularly when the appointment was made by one.

2 handling the dynamics of a couple, possibly arguing between themselves, contradicting each other and so on.

3 possible conflict of interests between husband and wife. This will depend on how much the wife actually knew.

4 dealing with the clients' concerns about confidentiality.

5 explaining to the clients why their actions are criminal.

## 7.4    Role-play 3

### Office memorandum for interviewer

You have an appointment with Vicky/Vic Mitchell who is very concerned about their landlord and the possibility of being turned out of their flat.

### Client role-play 3

You are Vicky/Vic Mitchell. Please supply details of address, phone number and job. You are either very anxious and distressed or angry because you are going to lose your home. As a result, you should present the information in an incoherent manner with interjections about 'unfairness', the 'uselessness of the law' and so on.

You arrived in the area about three months' ago and entered into 'a holiday tenancy agreement' with a Mr and Mrs Caleb Barkis. You don't know where they live but do have a 'phone number. The agreement allows for two weeks' notice by either party. You pay £80 per week inclusive of bills and the landlord collects the rent fortnightly. You do have a rent book. The house has four other bedrooms which are let separately to two couples and two singles and you all share the bathroom and kitchen.

Recently you had a phone call from British Telecom saying that the telephone bill had not been paid and you would be cut off. Two days ago, one of the other residents opened a letter in error. It was addressed to the landlord but was not marked private and confidential and was from solicitors acting for a building society. The letter said that a court order for repossession of the house had been obtained and they were waiting to hear from the landlord. You are very concerned about losing your home and the risk of bailiffs coming round and seizing your possessions. This happened to friends of yours in a similar situation and although their possessions were not seized because they were there at the time, they had to leave within the hour.

You also want your deposit returned (£160 ie two weeks' rent in advance). The next fortnight's rent is due on Friday and you are rather afraid of the landlord and do not want to reveal that you will be leaving. You do not want to cause any trouble because you like Mrs Barkis who has been very friendly and helpful. However, you are very worried about finding somewhere else to live, especially if you cannot get the deposit returned.

Essentially you want some advice about what to do with the minimum loss and trouble.

## Commentary for role-play 3

Unfortunately this kind of problem is not uncommon, where tenants find themselves the victim of a landlord who has failed to pay the mortgage and the house is therefore repossessed. Usually the building society is unaware that tenants are involved at all and they therefore have no protection against eviction.

1  This interview will test your skill in presenting 'bad news' ie that the client will lose his/her home. Do think about the practical and emotional effects of, potentially, not having anywhere to live. There is the additional fear of the bailiffs and the risk of losing one's possessions.

2  This interview should also give you some experience in dealing with an angry or distressed client.

3  Since there is no effective legal solution to this problem, were you able to offer any practical advice to assist the client immediately?

## 7.5 Role-play 4

### Office memorandum for interviewer

Mr/Ms Pat Stapleton has made an appointment to see you. Stapletons is a local family business that makes shelves and he/she is the manager. They have a problem with their manufacturer and distributor.

## Client role-play 4

You are Pat Stapleton and your family owns a business (Stapletons) that supplies shelving and storage systems. You joined the business a couple of years ago after doing a law degree and you help your father to run the office. The business has been trading for about 30 years and has a very good reputation.

You supply via distributors, mainly for domestic systems and the DIY market. Last year you went into office fit-outs as a new venture. One of your long-standing distributors (Derry & Co) asked you to supply shelving for a new office block.

You sub-contracted the manufacture of the shelf brackets to McKenzies who are specialists in glassfibre plastics and injection moulding. They have done this kind of work for you before but for much smaller components for domestic use. Although the brackets were made to your specification you have no expertise in a product of this size, its weight-bearing qualities and so on. It now appears that neither did the manufacturers.

The brackets and shelves were supplied to Derrys for a new office block. After a week many of the shelves collapsed and they all had to be replaced as quickly as possible so that the offices could function efficiently. The overall cost to Derrys was in the region of £45,000, including overtime for the fitters who had to work in the evening. Derrys claimed this sum from you and your firm took the commercial view that you should retain good relations with this long-standing distributor and pay out. You were also concerned to protect the reputation of your firm.

You have now approached the manufacturer to compensate you, but they deny liability since the goods were made to your specification. You of course relied on their expertise. The issue then is: whose responsibility was it to ensure that the brackets were strong enough to support the shelves under the weight of office equipment? While you know that this could be litgated, the whole affair has upset your father to such an extent that he has become ill. However, the business cannot afford this sort of loss and you therefore want to reach a settlement with the manufacturers but you do not want to go to court.

Please be prepared to supply addresses etc if necessary.

## Commentary for role-play 4

This is a relatively straightforward contract problem except for the question of responsibility for the design and fitness of the goods. You will probably not be able to advise at this stage on the client's chances of success in litigation.

1   What alternatives did you consider? For example, negotiating a settlement on the basis of shared or proportionate liability, or some other form of alternative dispute resolution?

2   The need to recover some or all of the money paid to the distributors should be weighed against the cost of litigation.

3   Another relevant factor is that this is a family business with a good reputation. The father's health and ability to run the firm is therefore important - a further reason to avoid litigation.

4   Bear in mind also the important commercial reality of maintaining good relations with the manufacturers and distributors.

# CHAPTER

## 8 Communication Skills & Career Development

This book has concentrated on developing communication skills in the context of client interviewing. However, such skills have a much wider application and even if you are not given the opportunity to interview clients yourself in the early stages of your career, you can learn from observing and evaluating the performance of others which is the next best thing to undergoing the experience yourself. You never stop learning.

Some not uncommon faults that even highly experienced lawyers still sometimes display include the following:

- not listening (lawyers prefer talking)
- interrogating by using largely closed questions in the mistaken belief that it is time-saving
- trying to solve problems on their own, for example failing to ask clients what they want
- offering advice before sufficient information has been obtained
- not testing the information (this is particularly true of the inexperienced - developing a certain amount of scepticism is useful).

Participating in role-plays whether as solicitor, client or observer provides good experience and accelerates learning. Giving and receiving structured feedback is an essential part of the role-play and will help to develop skills of self-assessment and assessment of others.

As your career progresses, you will find greater opportunities for putting the skills you have learned into practice in a wide range of situations.

## 8.1    Marketing and client care

As we saw in Chapter One, lawyers are running businesses and they now have to sell their services. One of the most effective ways of doing this is in the quality of the service you provide. This does not just mean legal competence but how the client is treated. While dissatisfied clients complain, satisfied clients will not only return but recommend you to others. It is therefore essential that everyone who has contact with clients understands this and is prepared to play a part in it. One of the most important skills in this process is effective communication.

For more junior solicitors and support staff communication is most likely to take place by telephone. Communication by telephone is particularly difficult because the only sensory perception available is hearing. This means that you have to be particularly careful about your tone of voice and the attitude you convey through it. Do you sound friendly, helpful and approachable, or irritated and impatient? Your facial expression and posture play a part in this. For example, if you smile you immediately sound warmer. Standing up rather than sitting hunched can help you to should assertive rather than defensive. You may well find that even as a junior member of the team you have to deal with a client on the telephone and it is therefore important that you create a good impression. The client will not be impressed by you saying 'I am only a trainee solicitor I'm afraid'; you are representing your firm and you can still take a message efficiently and make sure it is delivered to the appropriate person, even if you cannot (and would not be expected to) provide the answer yourself. It goes without saying that all telephone calls should be returned as promptly as possible.

## 8.2    Appraisals

At the start of your career, you will be on the receiving end of appraisals or reviews and should try and regard these as positive learning experiences, however inexpertly they may be delivered (see Giving and Receiving Feedback at paras 6.6 and 6.7 in Chapter Six). As you progress, you will be called upon to review the performance of others from time to time, for example, secretaries, trainees who are assisting you and, when you reach partnership, solicitors who are working with you. Listening, questioning and giving feedback are all of importance here if the appraisee is to learn and develop and also for their confidence and motivation. The review may take the form either of informal feedback at the end of a matter or a more formal interview perhaps on an annual basis. Make sure that you have a structure and always start by encouraging the appraisee to review his/her own performance first. Be prepared to listen and be brave but tactful about giving bad news. This does not mean ambiguity but it is important to think about how you present criticism in order to make it acceptable, and therefore remediable.

## 8.3 Recruitment interviews

Bearing in mind that an interview is a conversation with a purpose, you will only have a vague idea of the purpose of a job interview unless you have first drawn up both a job description and a person specification. You will then be able to structure the interview to discover whether the candidate has the qualifications, experience, skills and qualities for which you are looking. It is expensive and damaging to both sides to recruit the wrong person so it really is worth spending time on thinking, preparing and planning before you even select candidates for interview. Clearly you need to structure the interview and plan questions in order to achieve your objective in selecting the best possible candidate for that particular job.

## 8.4 Postscript

To communicate effectively is a most satisfying and marvellous achievement. It improves our relationships with others immeasurably. Effective communication skills are often underrated because it is taken for granted that we all communicate as naturally as we breathe. In practice, we know that this is not the case. I hope that this book will have encouraged your enthusiasm for learning to communicate better.

# Additional Reading

Developing and practising the skills essential for effective communication will help you to improve your ability both as an interviewer and a negotiator. Although there is no such thing as a model interview, there are a variety of 'models' and approaches, and it is important to develop your own style and be able to adapt it to different clients and situations. The following books will give you views from both the USA and the UK.

| | |
|---|---|
| Law Society (1993) | *The Guide to the Professional Conduct of Solicitors* |
| Gold, N, Mackie, K and Twining, W (1989) | *Learning Lawyers' skills* Butterworths |
| Twist, H (1992) | *Effective Interviewing* Blackstone Press |
| Sherr, A (1986) | *Client Interviewing for Lawyers* Sweet & Maxwell |
| Shaffer, T L and Elkins, J R (1976) | *Legal Interviewing and Counselling in a Nutshell* West Publishing Company |
| Binder, D A and Price, S C (1977) (1991) | *Legal Interviewing and Counselling - a Client Centred Approach* 1st edition - West Publishing Company 2nd edition (with Bergman, P) |